PRO~~VINCIAL GOVERNMENT~~

BANKS

PROVINCIAL GOVERNMENT BANKS

A Case Study of Regional Response to National Institutions

John N. Benson

Assistant Professor of Economics
University of Guelph

THE FRASER INSTITUTE
1978

Canadian Cataloguing in Publication Data
Benson, John Norman, 1942-
    Provincial government banks

    Bibliographical references included in
"Notes."
    ISBN 0-88975-020-3
    1. Banks and banking—Canada. 2.
Government financial institutions—Canada.
I. Fraser Institute, Vancouver, B.C.
II. Title.
HG2704.B45   332.1'0971   C77-002244-8

Contents

PREFACE

THE AUTHOR

AUTHOR'S INTRODUCTION

CHAPTER I:
PROVINCIAL OWNERSHIP OF BANKS:
AN HISTORICAL REVIEW OF THE DEBATE

CHAPTER II:
INTERPROVINCIAL DISCRIMINATION BY BANKS

CHAPTER III:
THE BANKS AND BRITISH COLUMBIA:
TESTS FOR DISCRIMINATION

CHAPTER IV:
ECONOMIC IMPLICATIONS OF PROVINCIAL GOVERNMENT OWNERSHIP OF BANKS

Preface

Background

This study was begun in 1975 with the objective of examining in detail the economic rationale for the proposal by the then government of British Columbia to establish a government-owned 'super bank' in the province. Although called 'British Columbia Savings and Trust' in the enabling legislation—to avoid the prohibitive provisions of the federal Bank Act—the proposed financial institution had the powers of a bank, as well as those of a trust company and, in addition, was enabled to provide insurance. Such a sweeping intervention in the institutional structure of the province clearly merited close scrutiny to determine the motives for undertaking it, as well as to assess its likely impact on the economic life of the province.

When the study had been partially completed, the NDP government called an election and was defeated. The Social Credit government, which replaced the NDP, showed no particular interest in the enabling legislation for British Columbia Savings and Trust. This lack of action has been widely interpreted as an indication that the current government will not, in fact, proceed with the creation of the super bank.

Under some circumstances that fact might have been enough to cause the Institute to abandon the study as redundant. However, such a decision was not made for several reasons. First of all, the establishment of B.C. Savings and Trust was not an isolated incident, but only the latest in a series of actions taken by several successive governments of British Columbia. Furthermore, the sentiments that, according to their own description, motivated the NDP government to launch B.C. Savings and Trust were very similar to those expressed by all four western premiers at the Western Economic Opportunities Conference, held in Calgary during June 1973. Accordingly, B.C. Savings and Trust should not be viewed, as it sometimes is, as the isolated action of one ideologically-motivated government, but rather as the expression of a long-standing and widespread disaffection for existing financial institutions. Since there have been no fundamental changes in existing institutions, it is reasonable to suppose that the origins of this disaffection remain. One purpose of this study was to ascertain the basis in fact for the sentiments that found expression in B.C. Savings and Trust and since such a documentation has never been provided—even by the NDP government that proposed the super bank—we decided to continue the research and publish the resulting book.

National financial institutions and the unity debate

A second and perhaps more important reason for proceeding with and, at this time, publishing the book has been provided by the current debate over national unity. Although the election of the Parti Quebecois in Quebec has focused the minds of Canadians on the country's institutions in a way unparalleled in the nation's history, that recent event is only one of a series that have tested the mettle of Confederation. The debate over revenue sharing in mining and energy resources, the extent of provincial jurisdiction in communications, the regional impact of federal trade and tariff policies and the long-standing debate about the control of financial institutions have all provided their share of federal-provincial tension in the past decade.

While most of the controversy has centered on particular policies of the federal government, many of them arise from a dissatisfaction with the institutional arrangements that are the result of federal policies. The federal Bank Act, for example, deals with the establishment and control of Canada's banks. It also contains explicit provisions governing the extent to which provincial governments can become involved in the ownership or operation of a bank. The fact that banks exist at the pleasure of federal legislation has, until recently, meant that full service banks have, by and large, been national institutions. As such, they have continuously had to fend off the attack that they discriminate amongst the regions of the country. Nowhere has this attack been more vociferous than in the West.

The interesting question that arises out of this particular controversy is the extent to which national institutions can function in a country as regionally diverse as Canada without *seeming* to discriminate amongst the regions. This distinction between diversity and discrimination lies at the root of many of the problems perceived to be associated with Confederation. For example, the evenhanded, national application of a particular policy either by the federal government or by a firm such as a bank may have different impacts in different areas of the country. That is only to be expected and should not be viewed as discriminatory behaviour even though it may be perceived as such by the various regions.

In his analysis of the motivation for the establishment of provincial government banks, Professor Benson carefully analyzes the phenomenon of discrimination both in principle and in a particular instance. Although the example chosen is British Columbia, the analysis is relevant for the much wider debate about the extent to which national institutions can effectively respond to regional needs and interests: hence the subtitle of this book, *A Case Study of the Regional Response to National Institutions.*

To underscore the relevance of this study for the current debate about the distribution of powers within Confederation, it is worthwhile listing the first two 'objects and purposes' of the B.C. Savings and Trust:

1. to encourage the citizens and institutions of the *Province* to deposit their funds to support further economic and social development of the *Province*, and

2. to ensure the maximum retention within the *Province* of the funds of the citizens and institutions of the *Province*.

A clearer statement of parochialism would be difficult to find—the question is, are the concerns displayed justified?

Do the banks discriminate against regions?

The bulk of Professor Benson's study is concerned with establishing whether or not the banks can or do discriminate against particular regions of the country. In Chapter two, he examines, analytically, the potential for discrimination. His conclusion is that "geographical discrimination by banks is unlikely to be significant or persistent." Ironically, Benson finds that the reason that discrimination is not likely, in principle, to exist is precisely because Canada's financial system is national in scope and highly integrated in character. The fact that national banks with branches nation-wide make up the payments system ensures rapid transfer of funds to and from regions in response to competitive pressures. If any one of these banks attempted to pursue a non-competitive policy and granted one region terms on loans or interest rates on deposits that were not in keeping with the basic economic situation in that region, other banks would, almost instantaneously, move to undercut the discriminating bank's position.

An interesting implication of Benson's analysis is that regionalization of financial flows may well work against particular regions. For example, the highly integrated nature of the Canadian financial system means that funds can and do flow freely to the regions where they can be most productively employed. The net effect of attempts to erect regional barriers to the free flow of funds—although designed to prevent outflow—may well be to interrupt required flows into the province. This is an important consideration—especially for high potential or fast growth regions which probably do not generate sufficient funds internally to serve their growth needs.

In Chapter three Professor Benson devised and applies several tests for actual discrimination to determine if the principles of Chapter two seem to be a good guide to 'real world behaviour'. He applies these tests to the particular case of British Columbia but the methodology and implications are clearly of interest for all regions of the country.

Professor Benson's conclusions are critical of methods that have been employed in the past to test for the existence of discrimination. In particular, ". . .a simple comparison of deposits and loans is not a valid test of discrimination." ". . .The provincial distribution of bank deposits and loans is not mystical or a matter of conspiracy. It is the natural consequence of funds in Canada moving in response to economic incentives and payments activities of the public."

Bank accounts reflect payment accounts

In isolating British Columbia's financial relationship with the rest of the country, Benson analyzes the trade and capital flows that lie behind payments to and from citizens of the province. He finds that, due largely to payments for services, B.C. has probably consistently had a net current account plus long-term capital account deficit with Canada and the rest of the world. That is, on balance B.C. residents consistently send more dollars out of the province for goods and services than are on balance received in the form of long-term capital flows from other Canadians and foreigners.

He also finds that bank assets outstanding in B.C. typically exceed liabilities outstanding, i.e., residents of B.C. borrow more money from the banks than they typically have on deposit. In other words, B.C. is a net borrower of funds.

"Chartered bank balance sheet data is, therefore, consistent with. . .British Columbia's trade and financial relationships with the rest of the world, including the rest of Canada. There is no evidence of discrimination in the sense that British Columbia's banking data is incompatible with what one might have expected on the basis of available information on the structure of the province's balance of payments."

Does British Columbia get an adequate share of the nation's money supply?

The lower level of bank liabilities relative to bank assets in B.C. may reflect a net outflow of bank deposits for payments purposes. On the other hand, deposits could be lower than loans outstanding as a result of discriminatory interest rate practices by the banks. That is to say, if interest rates on bank deposits were not as attractive in B.C. as they are elsewhere, total deposits at B.C. branches of the banks would tend to be low relative to other comparable regions. The question is, how do we assess the relative stock of deposits in B.C.?

In his analysis, Professor Benson relates British Columbia's share of total Canadian bank deposits to British Columbia's share of total economic activity. He finds that on average, British Columbia's share of total bank deposits exceeds by about one per cent the province's average share of Canadian economic activity. Because British Columbia's share of the money supply has exceeded the share enjoyed by the rest of the country, Professor Benson concludes that there is no evidence that interest rates on deposits have been set so as to discriminate against British Columbia.

The provincial government as banker—problem or solution?

In the final chapter, Professor Benson considers a range of objectives that might conceivably be pursued by a bank owned by a provincial government. "The general theme of the chapter is that a provincial (government) bank is not a costless remedy for the shortcomings provincial governments perceive in their provincial banking systems. Furthermore, the costs may be expected to rise sharply if provincial banks attempt to pursue credit policies which are misguided in terms of their understanding of the way the private banking system operates. The same competitive forces which mold the character of the operations of private banks across Canada will constrain the ability of a provincial bank to affect credit flows in the province and to confine the benefits and costs of its operations to residents of the province. On balance, it is difficult to be sanguine about the size of any net benefits which are expected to accrue to the province through the intervention of a full service provincial bank in the financial marketplace."

Among the objectives that might be pursued by a provincial government-owned bank, but which are considered to be invalid by Benson are: attempting to keep funds in the province, attempting to alter regional loan/deposit ratios or attempting to overcome perceived interprovincial discrimination by private banks.

Government banks and lower interest rates

One of the supposed advantages of a government bank is that it could provide borrowers with a lower interest rate than that provided by private banks. Professor Benson's analysis indicates that in most instances schemes designed to provide lower cost loans would involve subsidies—either explicitly or implicitly—and hence would be reflected in higher taxes. The only way that a government bank could provide generally lower cost loans without at the same time increasing taxes, would be if the government bank were more efficient than private banks. However, Benson is not optimistic that a government bank would be more efficient. Accordingly, he concludes that "taxpayers are well advised to ask the government how much owning a bank is going to cost and how such costs are to be financed?"

Amendments to the federal Bank Act

Benson's study does not support the contentions of those who, in the past, have suggested the establishment of banks owned by provincial governments. Accordingly, it provides interesting background against which to view the proposed amendments to the federal Bank Act. Current federal proposals would permit provincial governments to initially own up to 25 per cent of the voting shares of a new bank—declining to 10 per cent at the end of ten years. Since no single private owner of shares would be allowed to hold more than 10 per cent, the province's share, even after ten years, would enable it to have significant influence.

It is Benson's view that this partial ownership amendment (under current legislation provincial governments are only permitted to own non-voting shares) is likely to lead to problems of conflict of interest. To whom will the bank management defer—private or public owners? In Benson's view, this "uncertainty over partial government ownership could act to subvert the intent of the federal proposal since potential private investors are likely to be apprehensive over the possible deleterious effects of government influence on the new bank's performance."

Quite apart from his reservations about the technical features of the Bank Act revisions, Benson expresses grave doubts about dealing with the perceived problems in the context of existing legislation. The provinces already have the power to establish financial institutions that are banks in every respect except name (witness B.C. Savings and Trust) and any attempt to block provincial aspirations in this regard is bound to be frustrated.

In Benson's view, the "challenge then is to devise an institution which would permit provincial governments to enter certain aspects of the banking business so that they can pursue their valid intermediation goals while simultaneously removing the institution as a potential threat to the existing institutions and the stability of the Canadian fiancial system."

A solution?

"A possible solution would be to permit provincial governments to establish provincial banks under federal legislation separate from the Bank Act in the same way that the Federal Business Development Bank is handled. Restrictions could be placed on the functions and operations of such provincial banks to permit them to perform a gap-filling intermediation function without competing with existing institutions in credit markets presently regarded as adequately served. In addition, such a provincial bank's asset growth might be linked to net earnings performance. This would impose a limitation on the ability of the institution to take unfair advantage of its provincial government backing to engage in disruptive interest rate policies."

Diversity or discrimination? the unity debate

This study considers a very real and specific aspect of the sharing of regulatory power within Confederation. The results indicate that national policies, pursued either by governments or by private sector firms, may well produce different results in different regions. This regional diversity is often interpreted as discrimination and sometimes provokes regional policy responses. The rise of the concept of provincial government banks or near banks is one such response. This book shows that most of the regional concern in the case of banking is not justified and to the extent that it is justified, proposed remedies will not effectively provide solutions.

The Fraser Institute has been pleased to support Professor Benson's voyage into these important, but hitherto uncharted and hazardous waters. However, owing to the independence of the author, the views expressed by him may or may not conform severally or collectively with those of the members of the Institute.

M.A. Walker   **December, 1977**

THE AUTHOR

John N. Benson was born in Vancouver, B.C. in 1942. He received his Bachelor of Arts degree from the University of British Columbia in 1964, and his M.A. and Ph.D. degrees from Queen's University in 1967 and 1974, respectively.

After completing his course of study at Queen's University, Professor Benson joined the Department of Economics at the University of Guelph in the capacity of lecturer. Professor Benson's research interests being in the area of Canadian banking, he left academia for two years to acquire first hand experience with a banking institution. During 1972 and 1973 Professor Benson was employed by the Royal Bank of Canada and when he left in 1974 to return to the University of Guelph, was Senior Economist at the bank.

Currently, Professor Benson is Assistant Professor of Economics at the University of Guelph and is working on a text book to be published during 1978 by Methuen of Canada. His current research work relates to various aspects of the structure, operation and performance of the Canadian banking system.

AUTHOR'S INTRODUCTION

Motivation

This monograph is intended to contribute to the debate over whether provincial governments should own and manage banks or near banks. An independent economic study is needed to ensure that there is available a carefully thought out and well researched analysis of issues involved. Canadian chartered banks and other privately-owned deposit-taking institutions are the heart of Canada's system of payments and financial intermediation. Intervention by government which is predicated on a lack of confidence in the operations of these institutions is a serious matter and deserves careful study.

Provincial ownership of banks represents a specific type of intervention in Canadian financial markets. When a government proposes to intervene in this or some other way, the goals of such intervention need to be articulated as a necessary first step to effective policy formation. The next step is to decide whether government intervention is truly helpful in the achievement of these goals. The decision will depend partly on the form of intervention chosen by the government.

Whatever the technique or instrument chosen, it is rightly the subject of controversy and analysis. Some controversy will stem from matters dealing with analytical aspects of the effectiveness of the instrument in reaching desired goals. Often, however, controversy exists because one instrument is preferred above another by interest groups, the preference being based on psychological, philosophical, ethical or political preference. Whatever the instrument used, once it is put into place by the government, it is reasonably certain to remain unchanged for a long period of time. Change is difficult once the political, economic and institutional environment adapts to the government's presence.

1

Appropriate analysis is essential to a satisfactory resolution of the controversy or debate. This is where this study is viewed as fitting into the policy formulation process. Arguments which have been used both to assert and reject the need for provincial government ownership of banks or near banks have been based on wrong or misleading analysis and information. There is a need for a clear assessment of the economic justifiability of government concerns over the provincial effects of the operations of Canadian banks.

Discrimination?

This monograph attempts to contribute to the debate over provincial government ownership of banks and near banks by identifying and evaluating the economic validity of the major concerns of provincial governments regarding the operations of banks in Canada. Only one of the concerns, namely that banks discriminate unfairly among the provinces in the quality, cost and availability of the services they offer, is subjected to detailed examination. This is warranted in the light of the importance of this concern in the debate and the inadequate attention it has received hitherto. The analytical background that the examination of discrimination provides is valuable when evaluating the likelihood that provincially-owned banks or near banks will achieve objectives proposed for them by a provincial government.

A conclusion

A major conclusion of the study is that provincial government ownership of banks and near banks is not justified in Canada on the basis that banks discriminate unfairly against borrowers and lenders in different provinces. On the other hand, government intervention of some sort may be justified if the risk preferences and resulting portfolio policies of the banks are proven to be inimical to the achievement of economic and social objectives of a particular province. However, the judgement of this study is that a full service provincially-owned branch banking system is not an appropriate vehicle for pursuing those government objectives which are justified. A preferred solution would be to permit provincial governments to establish a more limited type of federally-incorporated banking institution outside existing chartered bank legislation.

The B.C. debate

The statistical analysis in the study focuses on data for the province of British Columbia. The reason for this may be of interest. Research for this study was initiated in the late summer of 1975 with the objective of contributing to the analysis of the economic justifiability and appropriate role of the British Columbia Savings and Trust Corporation. The latter crown corporation was established in May 1975 by the former New Democratic Party government of British Columbia and was scheduled to begin operation in 1976. The election of the Social Credit government in December 1975 in British Columbia has created uncertainty regarding the status of British Columbia Savings and Trust. It is not clear at this time whether the concept and objectives of British Columbia Savings and Trust will be embraced wholly or in part by the current government of British Columbia. Nevertheless, the debate over the need for government ownership of banking type institutions in Canada will continue. Although British Columbia statistics are used to test certain hypotheses about the provincial role of Canadian banks, the analysis in the study is of general applicability. It offers a framework for the analysis of the behaviour of the banks in all provinces and in so doing promotes a better understanding of interprovincial financial ties which bind the provinces together.

And the Bank Act too . . .

It is also hoped that this study will contribute to the current debate over the revision of the Bank Act slated for 1978.* In 1973, the federal government announced its intention to amend the Bank Act to permit provincial government ownership of the voting shares of banks. The recently

---

*The Bank Act is the federal statute under which private business firms calling themselves 'banks' must be incorporated. The Bank Act is revised and amended by Parliament every ten years. See Queen's Printer, *Bank Act,* 1966-67, c. 87, s.1.

published *White Paper on the Revision of Canadian Banking Legislation* confirms the federal government's intention in this regard. This study evaluates the federal government's recommended amendments pertaining to provincial government ownership of banks.

Structure of study

The study is organized in the following manner. Chapter I looks at the history of the provincial ownership debate as it applies to banks. The positions of the major protagonists in the debate are examined. Several concerns are seen to have been expressed by provincial governments about the operations of private banks. Discrimination has been a dominant one. The objectives of the British Columbia Savings and Trust Corporation are introduced and the evaluation of the legislation proposing its establishment is discussed. Chapter II addresses itself to an analysis of the possible nature of bank discrimination among provinces or regions in Canada within the context of the way Canada's branch banks operate in Canada's integrated financial markets. It is argued that banks are unlikely to discriminate between provinces. However, the possibility exists that bank portfolio policies regarding risk could result in differential impacts on the provinces in terms of the cost and availability of credit. Chapter III attempts to test for the absence of discrimination by examining banking statistics for British Columbia compared to the rest of Canada. It is stressed that the geographic location of deposits depends importantly on the chequing activities of the public. These in turn reflect millions of independent decisions on purchases of goods, services and financial instruments. Statistics on the provincial distribution of loans and deposits do not constitute a method of testing for discrimination. On the other hand, the structure of the British Columbia economy and the pattern of its economic relationships with the rest of the world suggest alternative explanations of banking system deposits and loan statistics. The latter are felt to be consistent with basic economic theory, and with the absence of discrimination. Chapter IV returns to the issue of provincial ownership of banks and evaluates the justifiability of such policies in the light of the preceding discussion of the nature of bank operations and their influence on the allocation of deposits across Canada. The chapter finishes by offering a few concluding comments and recommendations regarding the forthcoming Bank Act revision and the issue of provincially-owned banks.

Acknowledgements

I am indebted to the Fraser Institute for providing the financial support needed to carry out the study. Dr. Michael Walker, Research and Editorial Director with the Fraser Institute, had the unenviable task of editing, vetting and in general overseeing the task of producing the study. The Fraser Institute also arranged with Professors James W. Dean and Richard Schwindt of Simon Fraser University to provide me with statistical and other research materials which were essential to the successful completion of the study.

Extensive comments on an original draft were generously offered by a number of anonymous referees. One referee in particular helped enormously to place the subject into sharp perspective. In addition, I benefited from extensive discussions with Dr. J.W. Skinner, Dean of Social Sciences at the University of Guelph, as well as from access to material Dr. Skinner has written on government intervention in the monetary system. Finally, I appreciate the excellent research assistance provided by Miss Valerie Barnes and Mr. Richard Dologowski, economics students at the University of Guelph, who laboured in libraries and over calculators preparing much of the research material.

Chapter I

Provincial Ownership of Banks: An Historical Review of the Debate

Chapter I

Provincial Ownership of Banks: An Historical Review of the Debate

I. INTRODUCTION

Direct government involvement in Canadian financial markets is not a new phenomenon in Canada. This country has a long history of federal and provincial government involvement in financial markets. The consequence is that today these governments have considerable influence on the size and direction of the flow of funds in Canada through various government owned and operated financial institutions, industrial development programmes, government loan guarantees, government administered pension plans and bond issues.[1] Neufeld's 1972 study contains data which indicates that in 1969 approximately one-quarter of all Canadian assets of Canadian financial intermediaries were held by government institutions.[2]

The purpose of this chapter is to identify the motives which have prompted provincial governments to propose or establish government-owned banks.[3] To this end, it surveys the functions of provincial government banks which have existed from time to time in Canada, examines the debate over provincial ownership as it surfaced during the Western

Economic Opportunities Conference in 1973, and investigates the nature of the proposed British Columbia Savings and Trust Corporation. This information is sifted with a view to determining what exactly are the concerns that motivate provincial governments to consider the establishment of their own banks.

Early involvements—savings banks

Government ownership of banks and near banks existed as long ago as the 1830s when the governments of Newfoundland and Nova Scotia established savings banks.[4] The latter apparently provided savings facilities at a time when private savings institutions were still underdeveloped. These savings institutions were taken over by the federal government at the time of Confederation and, in 1929, absorbed into the Post Office Savings Bank which had been established shortly after Confederation in Ontario and Quebec. All federal savings banks disappeared from the scene in 1968 when the Post Office Savings Bank was dissolved.

In 1920 the governments of Ontario, Manitoba, and in 1938 the government of Alberta, ventured into the savings bank area. These institutions were provincially-incorporated. Ontario and Manitoba called their institutions 'Savings Offices' while Alberta decided to use the name 'Treasury Branches'. As of 1977 only the Ontario and Alberta institutions are still in operation. The Manitoba Savings Office closed its doors in 1930.

It is Neufeld's surmise that the Ontario and Manitoba institutions were established to fill a gap in the private market for agricultural credit which may have existed at that time. Funds deposited in these savings offices were intended to be funnelled into agricultural loans. Today the Ontario Savings Offices simply lend their funds to the Ontario Government for general spending purposes. Alberta Treasury Branches differ from the other government institutions mentioned by directly competing with deposit-taking institutions across a wide range of deposit, lending and financial services.[5] Alberta Treasury Branches are undoubtedly in the banking business.

II. RECENT PROVINCIAL INITIATIVES

In more recent years agitation for provincially-owned banks has been spearheaded by the Government of British Columbia. Fourteen years ago, in January 1964, the British Columbia provincial government, which was Social Credit at the time, announced its intention to promote the setting up of a bank under federal charter in which it would own 20 per cent of the shares. It argued that British Columbia suffered from not having a chartered bank with its head office in British Columbia. Existing chartered banks were felt to lack knowledge of British Columbia's economic situation. Proposed government participation apparently did not arise so much from a desire to manage the affairs of the chartered bank as to guarantee the success of its establishment by showing the public explicit government support for the bank.[6]

The government stressed the disadvantages of not having head offices of banks in Vancouver but had little complaint about the performance of the banking system. Attorney General Bonner in Senate hearings on the Bank of British Columbia said, regarding the private banks:

> ". . . legitimate competition. . .presently exists. Commercial banks compete with each other for accounts, and they do so in a variety of ways, all of which are proper, and upon which I offer no criticism whatever."[7]

Squelched in the Senate

The government was, therefore, arguing for a regional bank which would operate within the existing structure and practices of the private banking system. In October 1964, the Federal Senate Banking and Commerce Committee derailed the proposal. It recommended that the British Columbia plan not be proceeded with until the revision of the federal Bank Act, which was then underway, had been completed. The plan's death knell was sounded in February 1965 when the federal government announced its intention to pass legislation prohibiting ownership by any government of the voting shares of chartered banks and limiting ownership of non-voting shares to 10 per cent.

Such a provision was incorporated in a revised federal Bank Act passed by Parliament in the Spring of 1967. Chartered banks were prohibited from permitting the purchase of outstanding shares, or the subscription of new shares of their stock by federal, provincial or municipal governments. The provisions were not intended to include non-voting shares held in funds established to provide such services as medical care or pensions as long as the number of shares held does not exceed ten per cent of the outstanding shares. These provisions could be waived by the Governor in Council in the instance of the incorporation of a new bank.[8]

Private sector success

Although the provincial government's plans were thwarted, the push for a bank headquartered in British Columbia continued and bore fruit in 1968 when the Bank of British Columbia, the same one the British Columbia government had proposed four years earlier, was incorporated as a wholly privately-owned institution. Since that time the Bank of British Columbia has experienced extraordinarily rapid growth which suggests that government financing is not a prerequisite to success for banks operating on a narrow provincial or regional basis in Canada.

Western union on western needs

In June of 1973, the issue of provincial ownership of banks again burst before the public at the Western Economic Opportunities Conference held at Calgary, Alberta. There was a striking difference in the concerns expressed at this conference and those of the Government of British Columbia in 1964. At the conference a joint submission was made by the premiers of the four western provinces: Manitoba, Saskatchewan, Alberta and British Columbia.[9] This document launched a comprehensive assault on the chartered banks. The existing structure and operations of the banks were rejected as inadequate and a means of achieving direct government intervention in the banking market was proposed.

The provincial viewpoint

The following sample of quotes represents the view of the premiers:

> "The progress of development in Canada has been an east to west movement. But the pattern of settlement and development has been influenced by economic, financial and tax policies of the federal government, which early assisted the concentration of the nation's business and industrial activity in Central Canada. These policies which have led to this concentration of financial and industrial resources and of population have worked against the allocation of financial and production resources to bring balance to the economies of all regions of Canada. The Western Provinces wish to extend their frontiers and broaden and diversify their industrial base in order to increase job opportunities for their citizens today and in the future. Essential to this undertaking is an adequate availability of financial resources at competitive rates through institutions which are responsive to the particular needs of the Western Provinces. The branch banking system, characterized by the five major Canadian chartered banks with branches coast-to-coast and head offices in Central Canada, has not been adequately responsive to Western needs. (p. 3)

> ... The oligopolistic position of the Canadian chartered banks results in higher interest rates than are justified, a more conservative lending attitude, and less flexibility in their lending policy. (p. 4)

> ... The chartered bank's stimulation of development of Central Canada appears to have been done at the expense of the other regions of Canada. By mobilizing Western Canada savings and transferring them to Central Canada, the banks, in effect, have reduced the development potential of the West. The major portion of capital employed in the banking system represents

balances owing depositors rather than equity funds invested by shareholders. This is all the more reason investments should be made in regions in which deposits originate." (p. 5)

On the basis of these dissatisfactions the premiers recommended that the Bank Act be amended "to allow Provincial Governments to own and control existing, or to establish their own, chartered banks."[10]

Federal versus provincial perspectives

The brief of the provincial premiers contrasted sharply with the background submission prepared by the federal government for discussion at the Western Economic Opportunities Conference.[11] As might be expected, the federal brief takes a national perspective and stresses the importance of having nationally efficient capital markets. Chartered banks are viewed in this context as reasonably efficient financial intermediaries operating in a highly competitive environment with a branch system which has given Canadians many advantages in mobilizing funds across Canada.

A good illustration of the difference is offered by the following quotation which argues that a trade-off exists between the competition and other features of a financial system:

"Imperfections in a financial system such as the failure to respond to changing economic circumstances, uncompetitive institutional practices, oligopolistic pricing policies and excessively constraining government regulation will stand in the way of optimal performance. The fewer the frictions, the more efficiently the markets will function and the quicker they will respond to changing economic conditions. The cost of such frictions is in terms of misallocated resources, increased costs of credit and an unresponsive system. The key to their removal is lively competition in the services and prices available to savers, in the forms and costs of funds available to borrowers, and in other services available to the public. Competition may be restricted, not because of a conspiracy in constraint of trade, but because public regulation designed to protect the safety and liquidity of the institutions can produce results which inhibit competition. Consequently, emphasis should be placed on ensuring that regulations will minimize restraints on competition while at the same time providing for solvency and liquidity." (p. 8)

After looking at various aspects of the performance of the Canadian banking system, such as ability and success in competing internationally, its innovativeness, the need to compete aggressively with U.S. institutions, the great variety of services available and the probability that substantial economies of scale exist in branch banking, the conclusion was that the Canadian financial system (of which the banks are the dominant financial institutions) "is now operating in a highly competitive environment." (pp. 16-17)

Ambivalence on discrimination

The brief's review of the existence of unfair discrimination is more ambivalent. On the issue of the outflow of savings from western provinces the brief notes that:

"Although data on the financial system in Western Canada are incomplete, the evidence seems to indicate that the financial institutions and capital markets have channelled to borrowers in the western provinces as a whole a share of available funds larger than their proportions of national population and personal income. Broadly speaking this reflects the relatively high level of economic activity throughout the region, as well as the existence of special lending programs of particular relevance to borrowing needs in the four provinces. Over time, moreover, the financial institutions have expanded their range of activities and services and improved their ability to meet the growing financial requirements of business not only in Western Canada but in Canada as a whole." (p. 37)

However, the federal brief then proceeds to identify some problem areas. Notable among them is the problem of unfair

discrimination against the western provinces in the allocation of funds to meet regional credit and capital requirements. It attributes this concern to the fact that:

> "... head offices of major institutions are concentrated
> to a considerable degree in Toronto and Montreal, and
> this factor of location, together with the interlocking
> nature of the corporate business community, results in
> a lack of responsiveness to the needs for development
> capital in the West. In one instance at least, a provincial
> study has provided an estimate of an adverse balance
> between savings and loans in the province as evidence
> of an outflow of funds." (p. 47)

No analysis is made of the issue of discrimination. It is
simply reiterated that data is sparse and that:

> "To suggest that savings accruing within any one area of
> the country ought necessarily be reserved for use only
> within that same area would be as destructive of the
> concept of a common market within a country as would
> barriers restricting the movement of people and goods
> across provincial boundaries." (p. 47)

Other problem areas that were the subject of passing com-
mentary in the federal brief were the financing and management of small businesses, the concentration of decision
making centres in central Canada, the question of regionally-
based banks and the regional impact of national monetary
policies.

Regional banks viewed sympathetically

The brief is sympathetic to the view that the dispersal of
head offices across Canada and the establishment of regional banks might encourage development of regional money
markets and ancillary institutions in the major regional
centres. Since it is unlikely that existing banks would move
their head offices, the implication is that dispersal would be
achieved by way of the establishment of new banks. At the
same time the brief notes that:

"Generally it can be said that with the exceptions for provincial governments and non-residents noted above, there are no legislative restrictions hindering the establishment of new regionally-based chartered banks in any part of Canada. Moreover, the equity capital requirement of $1 million is relatively small and it would appear that the raising of such a sum is not a problem. What seems to be missing is the catalyst required to provide or insure strong promotion and good management." (p. 46)

Finally, it was noted that interregional differences in the impact of monetary policy had given rise to certain measures such as Bank of Canada 'moral suasion' to maintain the flow of bank credit to slow-growth areas and small businesses, and loan programmes of the Department of Regional Economic Expansion and guaranteed loan programmes of federal and provincial governments.

Bankers into the breach

In the face of the attack on the banks by the western premiers the chartered banks were not idle. Their industry association, the Canadian Bankers' Association, presented a brief at the Western Economic Opportunities Conference, which attempted to rebut many of the charges made by the western premiers.[12] In the Canadian Bankers' Association brief the advantages of branch banking systems are stressed and it is pointed out that, through their branch system, banks as employers, taxpayers, depositors, borrowers and shareholders, are intimately involved in, and contribute to, the economic life of the provinces. They argue that in their lending and deposit-taking activities they encounter intense competition. Also relevant is their argument that responsibility for meeting the financial needs of the provinces rests on the shoulders of a large number of private and government operated institutions. If the financial needs of Canadians are not being adequately met, why focus criticism solely on the banks? On the issue of head office location and the need for regionally-based banks they argued that:

"A continuous process of decentralization of authority has been going on for some years, and will continue in the future. Lending limits are substantially higher than previously and are constantly being increased. Decisions on loans of $1 million or more are now made in regional headquarters."[13]

Bankers deny deposit drain

In an attempt to repudiate the allegation that banks drain funds from Western Canada, the C.B.A. prepared, in their terms, an 'elegant study' which allocated the total domestic assets and liabilities of Canadian banks among each of the provinces. Subject to a number of difficulties in distributing the accounts, the statistics showed that as at October 31, 1972, assets exceeded liabilities in each of the western provinces by the following amounts.[14]

	($ million)
Manitoba	+ 205
Saskatchewan	+ 180
Alberta	+ 633
British Columbia	+ 207

On the subject of discrimination the brief concludes that "far from draining the Western Provinces the banking system places a higher proportion of loans in each province than the deposits it gains there."[15]

Federal government response

There was little public warning of the possibility that the federal government might change its policy on the issue of provincial ownership of bank shares. With the advantage of hindsight it now seems possible that the warning was contained in the weakly expressed support for the view that regionally-based banks might confer regional benefits combined with the expressed view that some type of catalyst is required. In addition it must be remembered that the Conference was held at the initiative of the federal government.

Quite predictably the premiers attacked the single most important set of financial institutions beyond their jurisdiction and under that of the federal government. Some response by the federal government was required.

The response took the form of an offer by John Turner, Federal Finance Minister at that time, at the Western Economic Opportunities Conference to amend the Bank Act so that one or more provincial governments would be permitted to put up a combined total of 25 per cent of the capital required to start up a bank. Over a period of several years the extent of government involvement would have to be gradually reduced to 10 per cent.

In mid March 1974, Bill C-13 was introduced into the Federal Parliament for the purpose of amending the Bank Act in the manner suggested by Finance Minister Turner.[16] The Bill died on the order paper of the Parliament in the Spring of 1974 when the federal government called an election.

Bankers bounce back

The banks were quick to respond to the July 1973 Turner announcement. In February 1974, in a thus far vain attempt to stop the proposal to permit government ownership of bank voting shares, the Canadian Bankers' Association again presented a brief to the federal government.[17] It first reiterates arguments about the 'deposit drain' allegation and then argues vociferously that vigorous competition already exists in the Canadian banking and financial system among government as well as private lending institutions and raises the possibility that provincial government ownership would reduce the effectiveness of federal monetary policy. In its critique of the implications of provincial ownership it raises a number of potential dangers which must be considered:

- political influence in decision making processes of a bank;

- further limitations on the effectiveness of monetary policy;

- political considerations might influence a bank's credit judgement to the detriment of shareholders;

- creation of conflicts of interest for government ministers;

- pressures on business to bank only with the government bank;

- public concern for privacy of their banking activities.

Bank Act proposals reproduce federal position

Apparently these arguments were unpersuasive. The recent *White Paper on Banking* has resurrected the provincial ownership proposal. It recommends that the Bank Act be amended to allow one or more provincial governments to hold up to 25 per cent of the voting shares of a new bank for ten years. After ten years this percentage would have to be reduced to 10 per cent.[18] This proposal is identical to the federal government's 1973 commitment. The rationale offered for the proposal is that:

> "It was established at the 1973 Western Economic Opportunities Conference that provincial governments might wish to assist through equity participation in facilitating the establishment of new banks. This proposal provides that opportunity."[19]

The proposed Bank Act amendments appear better designed to meet the demands of the government of British Columbia a decade ago than those enunciated by the provinces at the Western Economic Opportunities Conference. The western provincial governments wanted the right to establish a government-owned bank. Although the idea of providing 'seed' money may have been an important part of the 1964 drive for partial ownership rights by the government of British Columbia, in 1973 100 per cent ownership was the goal. If the federal government proved to be unwilling to go that far the provinces always have the option of incorporating under provincial legislation.

The Province of Manitoba has considered setting up a provincial institution. It noted in a 1973 report that:

"One way to provide for increased competition in financial markets and increased retention of funds within the province, would be to set up a public financial intermediary along the lines of Alberta's Treasury Branch system. Such an institution would accept deposits from the public, make loans to both the public and private sectors, perform a variety of services to the public (such as collection of utility bills and sale of various permits) and handle a large portion of government financial business.

The purpose of making commercial loans to the private sector is not to act as a lender of last resort, but to provide a degree of price competition to the banking system. A Treasury Branch operation would make a larger pool of funds available locally. Thus resident entrepreneurs would have an incentive to shop for financial services locally rather than in centralized markets outside of the province, or even outside of Canada. Not only would the Treasury Branch system help stem the drain of financial resources from Manitoba and make capital more accessible to local development, but competition in financial markets should also result in moderately lower borrowing costs to the consumer of commercial financial services. This would be of particular benefit to local businesses which often have a difficult time obtaining adequate financing from the banking system."[20]

British Columbia's second try

The Government of British Columbia went far beyond a statement of principle. On May 16, 1975 the then Premier of British Columbia issued a statement announcing the establishment of British Columbia Savings and Trust Corporation, a new financial institution to be incorporated in the province and controlled by the British Columbia government. The overall objectives of the institution were to:

"give the people of British Columbia a real alternative to the traditional types of financial institution that operate in the Province."

"to ensure that the financial sector in British Columbia has within it a strong public presence."[21]

The premier expressed confidence that the institution would ". . . contribute greatly to the economic and social development of our Province."

III. THE BRITISH COLUMBIA SAVINGS AND TRUST CORPORATION

British Columbia Savings and Trust was the first provincial saving and lending institution to be set up expressly for the purpose of competing with full service private institutions in forty years.[22] The New Democratic Party government which set it up foresaw its becoming operational in 1976. However, a provincial election in British Columbia in December 1975, which resulted in the defeat of the New Democratic Party government and election of a Social Credit government, has interrupted implementation of the enabling legislation. It is not clear at this time precisely what the new government intends to do with the structure, functions and objectives of British Columbia Savings and Trust. That the legislation has not been repealed suggests that the institution will continue to exist, and ultimately to operate but, perhaps, in a different way than originally conceived. (A more detailed examination of the scope and operations of British Columbia Savings and Trust is presented in Appendix I-3).

Arguments for a provincial bank?
In terms of the purpose of this study the legislation setting up the British Columbia Savings and Trust is valuable as it details the reasons why the corporation was set up. It is instructive to review them here. The goals of the company, listed as 'objects and purposes of the company' are:[23]

1. to encourage the citizens and institutions of the Province to deposit their funds to support further economic and social development of the Province,

2. to ensure the maximum retention within the Province of the funds of the citizens and institutions of the Province,

3. to attain a more equitable balance between loans and deposits among all regions of the Province,

4. to provide a full range of financial facilities and services,

5. to provide competition in the financial markets with a view to reduction of the rates of interest on borrowings by citizens and institutions of the Province,

6. to increase the availability and amount of credit for low-income and middle-income citizens, and to farmers, fishermen, and small businesses, and

7. to provide a full range of credit facilities and collection services, including the processing of payments to or from the Crown.

Objectives 1 and 2 reveal a concern over the flow of deposits between British Columbia and the rest of Canada. The implication is that deposits ('funds') are in some sense flowing out to the detriment of the province's economic development. Objective 3 is similar to 1 and 2 except that it is an intra-province concern. In a brochure entitled *British Columbia Savings and Trust* this objective is elaborated as follows:

> "Certain regions are poorly serviced by the existing large financial institutions. And in some degree the savings of the smaller areas are presently being used to finance investment in larger wealthier locations.

> A major objective of the British Columbia Savings and Trust will be to attain a better balance between loans and deposits among all regions of British Columbia.

> Funds raised in various communities will in large measure be used in those communities, and be re-invested into local economies."

This objective of improving the flow of deposits between the province and the rest of Canada and within the province seems based on the view that existing institutions, especially the banks, are in some sense discriminating against the province by pulling too much money out of it (or not putting enough in) and putting it into other provinces. Also that banks are discriminating against smaller communities within the province.

Objectives 4 and 5 reflect a desire on the part of the government, through British Columbia Savings and Trust, to increase competition in provincial financial markets across a broad range of banking services. Objective 6 implies that the government places a higher priority on certain types of loans than do the banks, given their risk/return preferences. Finally, objective 7 seems directed towards achieving a centralization of the government's existing financial activities and lending schemes with a view to improving their efficiency.

IV. SUMMARY

Although provincial governments in Canada are involved in numerous industrial development and specialized loan programmes their activities in the banking area have been quite limited. At various times Newfoundland, Nova Scotia, Ontario, Manitoba and Alberta have owned and operated provincial near banks. Their rationale was based upon the desire to fill in gaps perceived in the operations of existing institutions, especially as saving depositories and in the provision of agricultural credit. Today only Alberta's near bank offers a wide range of banking services.

Two features of the drive for provincial banks which gained impetus at the Western Economic Opportunities Conference stand out. First, the push for the right to have 100 per cent ownership and, secondly, the conviction that only a government-owned banking institution could rectify the hurts imposed on the provinces by the existing banking system. The 20 per cent ownership goal of 1964 is no longer satisfactory.

It would be easy to attribute this change in provincial demands to the political philosophies of three of the western provinces. In 1973 the governments of British Columbia, Saskatchewan and Manitoba were Socialist. However, such an attribution would contribute nothing to public understanding of the validity of the issues which are at the centre of the debate. And, in any event, the only province of the four with an operational provincial bank was the avowedly Conservative province of Alberta.

Several concerns may motivate provincial government intervention in banking regardless of the political persuasion of the party in power. This chapter has documented those concerns which have actually played a role in provincial government arguments favouring provincially-owned banks. Provincial governments which have resource or agricultural-based economies desire industrial diversification and industrial development ostensibly to provide employment opportunities. Governments apparently perceive benefits to the economy associated with lending to certain types of persons and businesses which are not shared by private institutions. They criticise the lending policies of nationwide banks as being too conservative, apparently feeling they do not lend sufficient sums of money to the right sorts of businesses. In addition, a number of provincial governments have expressed the view that the banks treat their provinces unfairly, draining deposits out of their province into others. In fact, the whole subject of the influence of banks on the allocation of funds is a source of great suspicion and concern—both within and between provinces.

Of the concerns enumerated, the matter of discrimination stands out as a prime target for careful analysis. This judgement is based on several considerations. Important among them is a conviction that the briefs of the provincial and federal governments, and the Canadian Bankers' Association, contributed little to an accurate understanding of the influence of the banks on the flow of funds between and within provinces. Because of the importance of this issue the next two chapters carefully investigate the matter of discrimination, emphasizing the situation of British Columbia—the province where much of the dissatisfaction emanated.

Related to concern over discrimination is concern that the banks are inefficient in the sense of charging higher lending rates than would exist in a more competitive environment. These rates have been viewed as incompatible with provincial government economic and social objectives. Insofar as the debate over provincial banking is concerned it is useful to divide the issue into two sub questions. Do chartered banks operate efficiently? Would an unsubsidized government-owned bank be likely to operate in such a way that it would increase competition in relevant lending markets to the net benefit of provincial residents?

This study makes no attempt to contribute to research on the first question. This reflects an appreciation of the complexity of the issue. Tackling it is beyond the scope of this book. The latest detailed study on competition among Canadian banks, *Efficiency and Regulation* by the Economic Council of Canada,[24] argues that competition among deposit-taking institutions in Canada should be increased with a view to reducing interest rate spreads. The latter report is unlikely to be the final word on the matter. In contrast the federal government, in its recent *White Paper on Banking,* did not display much concern over the economic power of the banks. No doubt the report of the Bryce Royal Commission on the Concentration of Corporate Power, currently in preparation, will address the issue of the structure and efficiency of the chartered banks. Instead this study limits its analysis to the likelihood that a government-owned bank would be successful in reducing loan interest rates on a provincial basis. This matter is postponed to Chapter IV— until the issue of discrimination has been dealt with.

Notes

[1]Some examples of each of these would be, the Central Mortgage and Housing Corporation, the Federal Business Development Bank, the Nova Scotia Industrial Estates Ltd., N.H.A. Mortgages, Farm Improvement Loans, the Canada Pension Plan and Canada Savings Bonds.

[2]E.P. Neufeld, *The Financial System of Canada,* Macmillan, Toronto, 1972, Statistical Appendix, p. 632.

[3]It is useful to dispense with a definitional matter. Canadian chartered banks are businesses which are incorporated as banks under the federal Bank Act. The Bank Act prohibits a business in Canada from calling itself a bank or describing its business as involving 'banking' unless it is incorporated under the Bank Act or permitted to do so by other federal legislation. Examples of the latter are the Bank of Canada and the Federal Business Development Bank. Near banks are deposit-taking businesses incorporated under federal legislation other than the Bank Act, or under provincial legislation, which consequently do not have the right to describe themselves as banks or their business as banking. They are, however, engaged in offering many of the same services as banks. *De facto* they are in the business of banking. Examples of provincial near banks are provincially-incorporated trust companies, credit unions, and mortgage loan companies. It seems widely accepted that the feature which businesses engaged in banking have which distinguishes them from other non-bank financial businesses is the right to offer deposits which are transferable to a third party. An alternative to using the bank/near bank designation in this study would have been to use the terms 'deposit-taking' or 'banking type institutions'. However, this was deemed to be terminologically confusing. Thus the terms 'bank' and 'near bank' are retained while recognizing the distinction is artificial from a functional point of view.

[4]This discussion of the early history of government intermediation draws heavily on Neufeld. See especially pp. 416-425.

[5]See Appendix I-1 and I-2 for a comparison of the sections of the Bank Act and the Act governing Alberta Treasury Branches which set forth the general functions of businesses incorporated under each.

[6]See Senate, Standing Committee on Banking and Finance, Hearings, 26th Parliament, Second Session. Wednesday, October 14, 1964, No. 3.

[7]*Ibid.,* p. 143.

[8]Bank Act, 1966-67, c. 87, s.1, sections 52 (1)(a), 53 (2)(3)(4), 54 (3)(c), 57 (1).

[9]Western Economic Opportunities Conference, July 24-26, 1973, Calgary, *Capital Financing and Regional Financial Institutions,* jointly submitted by Premiers of Manitoba, Alberta, Saskatchewan, British Columbia.

[10]The Joint Submission echoed sentiments expressed by the Manitoba government in a report published by that government in March 1973 entitled *Guidelines for the Seventies,* Vol. I, pp. 136-138. The latter report identified two major problems—a lack of competition among the chartered banks and outflow of funds from the province. It should be noted that the flow of funds criticism was levelled at trust and insurance companies (presumably national) as well as at the banks.

[11]Government of Canada, *Capital Financing and Financial Institutions,* prepared for the Conference on Western Economic Opportunities, Calgary, July 24-26, 1973.

[12]This was published in July 1973 as a special edition of a CBA Bulletin, *The Banks and the West: Facts, Figures and the Future,* Volume 16, No. 2.

[13]*Ibid.,* p. 9.

[14]*Ibid.,* pp. 4-8. A number of the statistical problems involved in interpreting provincial banking data were discussed by R.M. MacIntosh in an address at The Canadian Club, Winnipeg, Manitoba on April 5, 1973, entitled "National Banks and Regional Interests".

[15]*Ibid.,* p. 8.

[16]*Bill C-13,* 2nd Session, 29th Parliament, 23 Elizabeth II, 1974.

[17]Canadian Bankers' Association, *Governments' Place in Bank Ownership: The Industry View,* A Special edition of the Canadian Bankers' Association Bulletin, Volume 17, No. 1, February, 1974.

[18]*White Paper on Banking,* pp. 22-23.

[19]*Ibid.,* p. 23.

[20]Province of Manitoba, *Guidelines for the Seventies,* pp. 136-137. Another avenue to encouraging development of the provincial financial system considered by the Manitoba government is to strengthen "those financial institutions which fall within provincial jurisdiction, principally credit unions." See p. 137.

[21]British Columbia Government, *News Release,* issued by the Premier's Office on May 16, 1975.

[22]Budget Speech by the Honourable David Barrett, Premier and Minister of Finance, Friday, February 28, 1975, p. 23.

[23]To facilitate analysis the order in which the objectives are listed here has been changed from their order in the legislation. In the Act the following order was used: 4, 5, 1, 2, 3, 6 and 7.

[24]Economic Council of Canada, *Efficiency and Regulation: A Study of Deposit Institutions,* Ottawa, Canada, 1976, p. 2.

Appendix I-I

The Bank Act

BUSINESS AND POWERS OF BANK

General

75. (1) The bank may

(a) open branches;

(b) acquire, deal in, discount and lend money and make advances upon the security of, and take as security for any loan or advance made by the bank or any debt or liability to the bank, bills of exchange, promissory notes and other negotiable instruments, coin, gold and silver bullion and securities;

(c) subject to subsection (3), lend money and make advances upon the security of, and take as security for any loan or advance made by the bank or any debt or liability to the bank, any real or personal, immovable or movable property, except shares of the capital stock of the bank on which the bank has a privileged lien under subsection 83(1), but no such security is effective in respect of any personal or movable property that at the time the security is taken is, by any statutory law that was in force on the first day of July 1923, exempt from seizure under writs of execution;

(d) lend money and make advances without security; and

(e) engage in and carry on such business generally as appertains to the business of banking.

Source: *Revised Statutes of Canada, 1970,* Volume 1, Chapter B-1, p. 224.

Appendix I-2

Excerpt from the Treasury Branches Act

7. (1) Notwithstanding the terms and provisions of any contract, the Minister

(a)   may invest any moneys in the Fund in such securities and improved real property as he may prescribe and may from time to time vary and transpose any investments so made, and

(b)   may use any moneys in the Fund to make purchases of goods, wares or merchandise for resale on such terms as to payment as may be agreed upon.

(2) Subject to the regulations, the Minister

(a)   may loan any moneys in the Fund to persons, firms or corporations upon such terms as may be agreed upon, and

(b)   may take any security for any loan so made and may realize any security so taken.

[R.S.A. 1955, c.344, s.6; 1967, c.83, s.2; 1969, c.111, s.5; 1970, c.109, s.4]

Source: The Treasury Branches Act, R.S.A. 1955, c.344, s.1.

Appendix I-3

The British Columbia Savings and Trust Corporation[1]

The British Columbia Savings and Trust is a crown corporation of the province of British Columbia which was established in May 1975 by the provincial legislature to provide a variety of financial services to the provincial government and the general public within the province. It was intended to be either wholly-owned or predominantly owned by the British Columbia government. The British Columbia Savings and Trust has not begun operations nor has the present Social Credit government publicly announced its intentions with respect to the crown corporation. Thus a discussion of its nature must be somewhat speculative and based on the legislation which established it.

The previous New Democratic Party government invited credit unions in the province to purchase ten per cent of the company's twenty million authorized shares. The matter of credit union ownership and involvement has been contentious. It was hoped by the former British Columbia government that British Columbia Savings and Trust could be 'piggybacked' on top of credit union operations in the province. Purchase of shares of British Columbia Savings and Trust would involve a commitment by the credit unions. They would be expected to provide space in their existing 260 or so offices in British Columbia in which employees of the British Columbia Savings and Trust could offer the corporation's services to the public—an instant branch operation. In addition, the former government envisaged eight to fourteen regional offices in Vancouver, Victoria and other provincial centres.[2]

Its impact on the activities of other deposit-taking institutions in the province would depend partly on the amount of funds it is able to marshall for lending purposes. How large could the British Columbia Savings and Trust be? Initially the British Columbia Savings and Trust funds would be derived from the purchase of shares by the government and perhaps the credit unions along with the transfer of some portion of government cash and short-term investments from other financial institutions into British Columbia Savings and Trust. It may be that other crown corporations could also convert existing liquid assets into deposits at the British Columbia Savings and Trust.

The legislation setting up the British Columbia Savings and Trust provides for the issue of twenty million shares. Although their issue price has not been mentioned, taking a hypothetical price of $5 per share the sale of stock could immediately provide up to $100 million if the shares were all issued at once.[3]

Tables A-1 and A-2 show the dollar amounts and percentage changes in the cash and short-term investments held by the British Columbia government and its crown corporations, respectively at fiscal year ends (usually March 31), between 1968 and 1974. Since 1968 the total value of these liquid assets has averaged over $400 million. Clearly, the British Columbia government has at its disposal funds which, if deposited with the new 'bank', would permit the British Columbia Savings and Trust to grow quickly to the size of at least several hundred million dollars. These would be supplemented by additional borrowings by the British Columbia Savings and Trust in Canadian or foreign financial markets and by the growth of private deposits held at the institution if it proved successful in competing for deposits of other banking type institutions.[4]

APPENDIX TABLE A-1
British Columbia Government Cash & Short-Term Investments (STI)
1968-1976 (thousands of dollars) & Annual % Change
(End of Fiscal Year Figures)

	Cash[1]	Annual % Change	STI	Annual % Change	Total	Annual % Change
1968	20,304		157,408		177,712	
1969	34,546	70.1	193,825	23.1	228,371	28.2
1970	20,946	−39.4	78,934	−59.3	99,880	−56.3
1971	22,723	8.5	130,628	65.5	153,351	53.5
1972	22,483	−1.1	136,300	4.3	158,783	3.5
1973	27,016	20.2	196,687	44.3	223,703	40.9
1974	31,893	18.1	254,065	29.2	285,958	27.8
1975	28,422	−10.9	228,144	−10.2	256,566	−10.3
1976	15,050	−47.1	30,261	−86.7	45,312	−82.3

[1]Includes: cash on hand, cash in chartered banks in Canada, cash in banks in England (converted at rate for the year) and cash in United States banks (U.S. dollars).

Source: Public Accounts of British Columbia, 1968-1976.

APPENDIX TABLE A-2
Cash & Short-Term Investments in British Columbia Crown Corporations, 1968-1976
(thousands of dollars)
(End of Fiscal Year Figures)

	Cash	Annual % Change	STI	Annual % Change	Total	Annual % Change
1968	13,330		272,218		285,548	
1969	26,067	95.6	273,110	0.3	299,178	0.8
1970	24,198	−7.2	321,644	17.8	345,843	15.6
1971	28,231	16.7	342,447	6.5	370,677	7.2
1972	14,963	−47.0	438,242	28.0	453,205	22.3
1973	19,925	33.2	485,616	10.8	505,541	11.6
1974*	46,336	132.5	192,668	−60.3	219,003	−56.7
1975	102,655	121.6	178,267	−7.5	280,922	28.3
1976	148,224	44.4	172,248	−3.4	320,471	14.1

*No figures available for Workmen's Compensation Board for 1974.
Source: Public Accounts of British Columbia, 1968-1976.

Just as one cannot help but be impressed by the potential size of British Columbia Savings and Trust, the proposed scope of the corporation's operations arouses a measure of awe as well. As a financial intermediary its powers encompassed those of the chartered banks and other banking type institutions in terms of their demand, savings and notice deposit-taking and personal, business and mortgage lending activities. In addition, the British Columbia Savings and Trust was given the power to act as an agent for the province itself, any other public bodies or persons, and to appoint agents to act on its behalf, to act as a trustee, etc., etc. including, as the 25th power listed, the authority to "carry on the business of insurance in the areas of mortgage insurance, guarantee insurance, or credit insurance as defined in the Insurance Act." The legislation also provided for provincial government guarantee of the company's deposits and, upon approval of the Lieutenant Governor in Council, the guarantee could be extended to other forms of borrowing (notes, bonds, debentures and other securities) up to $100 million.

The British Columbia Savings and Trust was, consequently, a potential 'super bank', possessing within the province all of the powers of a bank plus many powers of other institutions such as trust companies. Although the former N.D.P. government reserved the bulk of its criticism for the banks, the intention was clearly to involve the British Columbia Savings and Trust in other areas, such as operating trust facilities. Criticisms which the former government had of the chartered banks were implicitly and quietly extended to other participants in the British Columbia financial system. One of the objectives of the British Columbia Savings and Trust was "to provide a full range of financial facilities and services." If the British Columbia Savings and Trust is in fact launched under its unamended original Act of Incorporation the adjective 'full' should be given a very comprehensive interpretation.

Notes

[1]Unless otherwise noted the details mentioned in this section relating to the structure, functions and objectives of British Columbia Savings and Trust are extracted from the relevant sections of Legislative Assembly of British Columbia, (Bill 86), Savings and Trust Corporation of British Columbia Act, Fifth Session, Thirtieth Parliament, 24 Elizabeth II, 1975.

[2]This information was reported in the Vancouver Sun, June, 1975.

[3]By way of comparison, the Bank of British Columbia has one million shares authorized of which 511 thousand have been issued at a par value of $10 each.

[4]On March 31, 1974, 58 per cent of the government's cash and short-term investments of $286 million or about $165 million was held at chartered banks. Since one of the objectives of the British Columbia Savings and Trust involves the processing of payments to or from the crown it can be expected that as the government moved to using cheques on deposits at British Columbia Savings and Trust as a means of paying bills, salaries, etc., much of these chartered bank investments would be transferred to British Columbia Savings and Trust.

A comparison with the Bank of British Columbia serves to impress one with the potential initial size of the British Columbia Savings and Trust. The Bank of British Columbia recorded total assets of $34 million on October 31, 1968, which was its first year of operation. By October 31, 1974 it had grown to about $480 million.

Chapter II

Interprovincial Discrimination by Banks

Chapter II

Interprovincial Discrimination by Banks

I. INTRODUCTION

Canada is a diverse country. Its geography, society, culture and politics differ between regions and provinces. Its economy, too, is varied reflecting the uneven distribution of natural, capital and labour resources across the country. Canada's financial system is not immune to these influences. A provincial cross-section of the financial system would reveal striking differences among financial institutions in the composition of assets and liabilities, growth rates and size from province to province. As is implied, such interprovincial differences are not fortuitous. They reflect heterogeneous financial legislation, different cultural and political attitudes and, most importantly, interprovincial differences in economic structure, growth, behaviour, opportunities, and hence financial needs.

Provincial governments are not immune to these influences either. It is, therefore, not surprising that a number of provincial governments find themselves dissatisfied with national chartered banks which appear to them to be at best provincially indifferent, at worst provincially discriminatory.

Diversity or discrimination?

One of the challenges Canadian diversity creates for national institutions is the need for them to deal with citizens in an evenhanded, non-discriminatory manner regardless of their geographical location. To do otherwise is to risk the embarrassing loss of goodwill and confidence on the part of the public they serve. The review of the debate over provincial ownership in the previous chapter revealed that concern does exist about the evenhandedness with which banks operate across Canada. Governments of western provinces, especially British Columbia, have alleged that banks do discriminate against their provinces to the benefit of central Canada. Unfortunately, the protagonists in the debate have not always articulated clearly the rationale behind their claims and counter claims about the existence and nature of discrimination.

What does the term 'discrimination' mean in terms of the geographical impact of banking operations? For the purposes of this investigation, discrimination is said to occur when the activities or policies of banks deal differently with bank customers in one or more locations compared to the same type of customers elsewhere. A measurable consequence of discrimination is that the distribution of funds and availability of bank credit within the economy is skewed or distorted compared to what might be expected in the absence of discrimination. Discrimination is not said to occur when the uniform application of nationwide, standardized policies by the banks has a fortuitous or incidental geographical impact. In other words, the view is rejected that discrimination by banks exists when they follow national policies which by nature are not well suited to all of the needs of each province or community.

In an attempt to clarify the economic issues involved, this chapter identifies and discusses three types of discrimination: administrative, price/non-price and credit rationing. These are felt to subsume key procedures and policies of the banks which are amenable to discriminatory application among different parts of the country. The primary objective of the chapter is to evaluate the likelihood that these forms of discrimination do constitute a threat to bank customers in one area compared to others. This evaluation is carried out in the light of relevant aspects of bank operations and the existence in Canada of a common currency system and a highly integrated financial system.

II. ADMINISTRATIVE DISCRIMINATION

It seems reasonable to define administrative discrimination as geographical differences in the quality of service offered to bank customers arising from the administrative practices, decision making procedures, and programmes offered by a bank. Many of the concerns which might be construed as involving administrative discrimination can be dredged up from the classic debate in banking literature over branch versus unit banks. An example would be concern over the possible lack of responsiveness of branch managers to the local lending needs of smaller rural communities (or provinces). The counter argument stresses the better professional training available to managers in a large branch bank. Branch managers will tend to be more aggressive, innovative and shrewd judges of credit worthiness. The consequence might well be lower lending rates for all borrowers due to the branch bank's lower loan losses.

The head office location issue

Concern over administrative discrimination in the context of the debate over provincially-owned banks in Canada has focused on the matter of the concentration of bank head offices in Ontario and Quebec. Such questions arise as: do loans from Western or Maritime provinces require a longer time to be processed in a bank with an Ontario head office than if the head office was in a western centre, or are they processed as rapidly as similar applications from Ontario customers?

No data are available which would permit an empirical analysis of this sort of question. However, the probable result of such an investigation can be inferred by an understanding of how branches operate. Each branch is run as a profit centre. The manager and employees work to obtain as many deposits and make as many loans as possible within the rules, procedures, and policies laid down by head office. A manager's future in the bank depends upon his success in building the bank's business. He would be the first to complain if he felt the procedures of the bank prejudiced his opportunities for advancement simply because of his

41

geographical location. Thus competitive forces *within* national branch banks tend to ensure that branches in all regions have equivalent opportunities to serve customers.

Furthermore, there are no technical reasons having to do with speed of communication or transfer of documents that would act to create discrimination. Perhaps, many years ago, when communications and mail systems were primitive, differences may have existed in the length of the administrative lag experienced in processing business among branches in different areas of the country. Not so now with telephone, teletype, telecopiers and internal mail service within each bank that guarantee minimal lags regardless of where a branch is located. The inference of these considerations is that loan applications tend to be processed in a similar manner regardless of where they originate.

Loan authorizations

Another aspect of concern over head office location involves the role head office plays in the authorization of loans. The function of the branch system has been recently described as entailing a network of small retail outlets which collect personal savings deposits and extend consumer loans.[1] Larger branches operate in wholesale financial markets collecting large size term deposits and extending industrial and other non-personal loans. A 1974 sample of 10 per cent of chartered bank branches revealed that 496 branches (of 629 branches in the sample) with deposits of less than $10 million held about 53 per cent of personal savings deposits and 56 per cent of personal loans. In contrast, the remaining 133 branches held 86 per cent of other term deposits and 86.5 per cent of industrial loans. These findings are consistent with those of the 1964 Royal Commission on Banking and Finance. It determined that although 96 per cent of loan accounts were handled solely at branch level these accounts amounted to only 31 per cent of loans outstanding.[2] Conversely, less than 4 per cent of accounts accounting for close to 70 per cent of loans were handled by regional or head offices.

42

These data suggest that head offices in the past have exercised a major role in loan authorization procedures associated with a bank's larger accounts. Proof of the existence of administrative discrimination would require more evidence than simply that, for example, businessmen in British Columbia feel the national banks are sluggish and uninterested in serving their financial needs. This information must be coupled with evidence that businesses in other regions, especially the head office region, receive qualitatively better treatment—more rapid, enthusiastic processing of the loan.

The most attractive opportunity
Here again it must be kept in mind that a bank is in business to earn profits—and hopefully higher profits than its major competitors. Within the province, branch managers and regional managers will push those accounts they regard as attractive to the bank. The perspective of head office will be different. Loan applications which get to head office compete with attractive loans emanating from branches and districts across the country. Thus, a loan to a firm in Hamilton, Ontario may appear attractive in terms of lending opportunities in the Hamilton area, but it could be less attractive than an alternative loan opportunity in Vancouver, British Columbia which is only known to head office personnel. If large bank customers perceived their financial needs from a parochial perspective they may misinterpret an adverse decision on a loan application by the bank's head office. What may be interpreted as a lack of understanding of the potential of a business simply reflects the existence of even more attractive loans elsewhere.

Discrimination unlikely
These comments do not mean that administrative discrimination does not exist. They simply suggest it is unlikely to be a significant phenomenon and that in some cases where bank customers feel they observe discrimination they are, in fact, observing the result of a prudent judgement among alternative lending opportunities. That administrative discrimination is not totally non-existent may be inferred from the fact (noted in the previous chapter) that the

Canadian Bankers' Association has recently suggested that banks are progressively decentralizing decision making authority.[3] This is presumably at least partly in response to net benefits which the banks perceive accruing from such decentralization. (On the other hand, the banks' move to permit more autonomy at regional headquarters may be cynically viewed as a response to political pressure and the threat of regional banks.) Among other things, decentralization reduces the probability that administrative discrimination will occur.

In its brief on the current Bank Act revision the Canadian Bankers' Association presented the following proposal to permit the banks to set up regional subsidiaries:

"The proposal put forward here represents the result of a search for a more flexible vehicle to enable the banks to adapt more closely to the need for specialized services in individual regions of the country and for organizations to provide specialized functions of general importance.

The organizational structure now decreed for the banks in the Bank Act prevents any further meaningful decentralization of operations or specialization of functions, and a new device is required to overcome present restrictions. For regional purposes this should be one that would permit further attention to the business demands of the area and also would assist in meeting the aspirations of people in different parts of Canada. For specialized functions of general importance it should provide a corporate structure in which the required skills and resources would be concentrated.

To provide such a vehicle we are asking that the banks be given the power to establish wholly-owned subsidiaries through which any of their permitted activities may be conducted. This freedom could be utilized in several ways. One of these would be the establishment of regional full service banking corporations. Special functional subsidiaries could also be established for leasing, factoring, consumer lending, mortgage lending and so on.

It is not suggested that the banks should be required to establish such subsidiaries but rather that they have the freedom to do so if it appears to serve certain markets or provide certain types of service *more efficiently and more acceptably to the public.*"[4]

Thus the banks have admitted publicly a certain amount of difficulty in custom tailoring their operations to provincial or regional needs. One interpretation of this is that provinces which have less specialized banking needs or which in some sense more closely fit the banks' standardized programmes do receive a set of banking services more appropriate to their requirements.

Manifestations of discrimination

From an analytical perspective, the consequence of administrative discrimination would be to increase the time and effort required to obtain loans by those borrowers who have been discriminated against. It could manifest itself in the slower growth of loans in those banks and in those geographic areas where discrimination is experienced. There would also be a tendency for loans at competing institutions which manage to avoid such administrative problems to grow more rapidly than would otherwise be the case.

III. PRICE AND TERMS DISCRIMINATION

This type of discrimination is said to exist when banks establish geographic differentials in the terms and conditions on which they are willing to make their services available. In economic theory, price discrimination is said to exist when the seller of a product is able to establish and maintain different prices for different customers for the same product where the differences in price do not reflect differences in production costs. The rationale behind price discrimination is that the seller is able to increase profits by charging different groups prices based on the willingness of those groups to pay. This contrasts with a situation where it is not possible to separate markets. In the latter case, arbitrage by customers will ultimately force prices to equalize so that only one price prevails. When a business successfully engages in price discrimination the customer paying the higher price is naturally regarded as being discriminated against.

Risk, cost and discrimination

In banking, interprovincial price discrimination would exist if depositors in different regions are offered different interest rates and service charges or borrowers face different interest rates and other loan contract provisions such as collateral requirements, minimum repayment periods and compensating balance requirements. In addition, before it could be said that discrimination exists, it would have to be demonstrated that these differences do not arise from interprovincial differences in risk and cost.

This latter *caveat* is an important one. Interest rates and other terms and conditions attached to the same types of loans can differ should the bank evaluate the expected profitability of the loans differently because of differences in costs or risk. Thus loan applications from businesses with a good record of profitability, good economic prospects and good history of loan repayment can be expected to enjoy lower interest rates and less stringent terms and conditions on their loans. Such loans would be regarded as having a higher expected profitability than those of businesses characterized by a spotty repayment record. Quite apart from offering lower expected profitability, because of higher risk of default on interest and principal, higher risk loans typically require more careful and expert investigation of the customer, proposed use of borrowed funds and the supervision of collateral. For example, personal loans are generally regarded as being higher risk as well as more expensive to administer than industrial loans. Therefore, the existence of higher interest rates and relatively less favourable non-price terms on personal loans would not constitute discrimination.

Barriers to discrimination

What is the likelihood that Canadian banks practice price and non-price discrimination on a geographic basis in Canada?[5] The biggest obstacle to success in geographic discrimination would be the high degree of integration which characterizes the Canadian financial system.[6] Integration exists when the set of institutional arrangements, the variety of sources of funds, and the degree of competition among market participants is such as to promote a high degree of mobility in the flow of funds in the financial system. In a highly integrated system funds flow easily and quickly in response to interest differentials and in the process tend to bring about interest rate equalization.[7]

The Canadian banking and financial system is bound together by an efficient payments system, sophisticated information and communications systems, and the freedom of borrowers and lenders to search out the best terms and conditions on which to obtain funds or put them to use. The payments system refers to the facilities offered by the banks for the physical clearing of cheques and other types of transfers from one location to another. Near banks also offer payments facilities on a nationwide basis, where necessary using the banks' clearing system on a fee for service basis to facilitate near bank customers' chequing activities. The great efficiency of our payments system guarantees the quick transfer of funds to and from every corner of the country. As a direct consequence, transactions can be settled quickly and persons with surplus funds can search out attractive lending opportunities with a minimum of difficulty.

At the same time sophisticated information and communications systems guarantee the instant availability of information on bank interest rates and service charges. The existence of higher rates on deposits in Ontario compared to British Columbia will induce inflows of deposits and wipe out the differential. This is not to say that it is impossible for any interprovincial differences in interest rates to exist. To the extent that circumstances exist which encourage distinct markets or financial instruments in the various provinces, differences can arise on at least a short-term basis. An example of a special circumstance would be the time zone differentials which exist across Canada. When Ontario and Quebec financial markets shut down in the afternoon, Eastern time, British Columbia markets remain open for another three hours. During those three hours market conditions in British Columbia can bring about interest rates different from those which prevailed earlier in the day in Ontario. Such differences, however, would be temporary and would tend to be wiped out the next day when the Ontario market opens. Borrowers in the British Columbia market paying higher rates on money market borrowings would search out the lower Ontario rates. Banks would not experience a persistent continuing opportunity to exercise price discrimination because of time zone differences.

Clearly, it will be difficult for banks to quote persistently different rates between different provinces or regions in Canada. Bank customers would be quick to learn about and react to any significant differences in lending or deposit rates. The Canadian Bankers' Association has claimed that "Through their nationwide branches the banks serve every region of the country with the same level of service, at the same charges and on the same terms."[8]

Less than full information?

Although information can be communicated instantly between different locations in Canada, information which is not publicly available will not be readily communicated. The claim of the Canadian Bankers' Association quoted above would be more reassuring if the actual charges and terms offered customers in each region were not confidential. What is in the public domain are a bank's posted rates. Thus customers are aware of posted deposit rates, posted prime lending rates and posted service charges. However, the actual rates charged may be different from posted rates. They are subject to negotiation between the bank manager and the individual customer. Even though branch managers operate within the framework of national lending policies it is conceivable that they are capable of negotiating loan terms in one location which may be more favourable to the bank than those on a similar loan negotiated elsewhere. Similarly, head office officials might negotiate terms more favourable to the bank on a large loan for a corporation in one area than in another.

Quite apart from the practice of price discrimination as a matter of general bank policy, could the aggressive pursuit by individual branch managers and other lending officers of maximum bank profits develop into an effective system of price discrimination? If borrowers search out the cost of alternative sources of funds, such as loans from other banks and near banks, directly issuing paper in the money market, obtaining trade credit from major suppliers and selling off previously accumulated assets, they will be able to establish the reasonableness of the terms they are being offered. The less informed the borrower, the less willing he is to consider alternatives, the fewer the alternative sources of funds available to him and the more urgent his need for funds, the more likely a bank will be successful in negotiating a preferential rate. On the other hand, bank managers have to view their search for profits in a longer term context. They want to attract customers who can offer the bank the prospect of a continuing, growing and profitable relationship over many years. Short-term exploitation of opportunities for price discrimination run the risk of losing the borrower's goodwill, and hence business, if over time the borrower discovers he has not been as well treated as he, with hindsight, might have expected.

Evidence from mortgage rates

Is there any independent evidence that interest rates tend to be equalized across the country for loans of the same quality? Unfortunately, few statistics on provincial interest rates are published. One series of rates which is published on a provincial basis is interest rates on N.H.A. loans. These are shown for the western provinces and Ontario and Quebec in Table 1. Interest rates on N.H.A. loans appear to vary, on average, a maximum of about one-tenth of one percentage point among the various regions of Canada and tend to be highest in British Columbia and Ontario. Since N.H.A. mortgages are guaranteed by the federal government this differential would not represent risk differences. One explanation could be that British Columbia and Ontario experienced stronger demand for mortgages over the years 1970 to 1976 than did the other regions. It must also be recognized that a differential of one-tenth of a percentage point is not large.

TABLE 1
Interest Rates on N.H.A. Loans for
New Housing by Approved Lenders
Annual Averages of Monthly Data, 1970-1976
(per cent)

	British Columbia	Prairies	Ontario	Quebec	Atlantic Provinces
1970	10.10	10.05	10.06	10.01	10.02
1971	9.08	9.00	9.09	8.98	9.02
1972	9.03	8.93	8.96	8.89	8.95
1973	9.51	9.39	9.42	9.30	9.48
1974	10.93	10.78	11.00	10.66	10.79
1975	11.21	11.02	11.22	11.02	10.99
1976	11.78	11.71	11.65	11.75	11.74
Average	10.23	10.13	10.20	10.09	10.14

Source: Central Mortgage and Housing Corporation, *Canadian Housing Statistics*, annually, 1970-1976.

Data on N.H.A. and conventional mortgage rates for houses and apartments, published by the Mortgage Insurance Company of Canada, suggests that a more sizable differential exists between large urban centres and more remote, smaller communities.[9] For example, Timmins frequently records mortgage rates one-quarter to one-half of a percentage point above Toronto rates. Yet, rates in Vancouver and Toronto are about the same, while rates in the Okanagan Valley in British Columbia are reported as frequently being one-quarter of a percentage point above Vancouver rates. It seems, then, that interest rate differences (though small) exist to a greater extent on an interregional basis than on an interprovincial basis in Canada.

To summarize, given the efficiency with which payments can be executed and widespread knowledge of interest rates in major bond and money markets and of the posted rates of the major lending institutions, significant interest differentials associated with successful price discrimination are unlikely to exist in Canada. As a final note it should be pointed out that if banks did act as profit-maximizing price discriminators it is not clear *a priori* which provinces would be confronted with the less favourable terms on deposits and loans. Price would be established on the basis of different demand conditions for different types of loans in the various regions. For example, loan interest rates would be higher in regions in which loan demand is less responsive to changes in price. There is no reason to think this is necessarily the case in the western provinces.

IV. CREDIT RATIONING DISCRIMINATION

Credit rationing discrimination concerns lending policies of banks. It refers to the application of loan quality control criteria or standards by the banks in a geographically discriminatory way. What types of businesses is a bank prepared to lend to? Are arbitrary maximum limits placed on the size of loans banks are prepared to make such that the borrower, after receiving the loan, still has an unsatisfied or excess demand for credit?

The need for credit rationing is evidence that banks are not perfect price discriminators.[10] If banks could perfectly price discriminate then excess demand for loans would not exist. There would be no need to ration credit, that is, to supply less than the amount the borrower demands under the conditions provided by the going interest rate and non-price terms. Difficulties in discriminating on a price basis lead to the need to establish common prices for customers with different demands for loans. A common rate will normally mean some borrowers can obtain as large a loan as they desire while others will want loans larger than the profit-maximizing bank is prepared to offer. In the latter instance credit rationing could take the form of arbitrary limits on the size of loan the bank is prepared to provide based on the bank's view of the quality of loans they are prepared to deal in.

Credit rationing discrimination would require that banks satisfy less of the demand of a borrower at going rates and terms in one part of the country than in another. Borrowers who were being discriminated against would experience relatively larger unsatisfied demands for credit. In the light of the standardized credit policies followed by branch managers, discriminatory rationing of borrowers would be unlikely to occur on small loans. This type of discrimination could be more effectively handled at head office where it would be easier to favour the availability of credit to borrowers in one region compared to another.

Why a bank would want to engage in this type of discrimination is not clear. It would not seem to offer the prospect of increasing the bank's expected profits in any obvious way. Indeed the latter could fall due to the administrative costs of implementing the scheme. Credit rationing discrimination would exist if head office lending officers for psychological, cultural, or political reasons (i.e. reasons other than the basic quality and risk characteristics of the loan) felt it was important to take care of central Canadian borrowers first. In this respect credit rationing discrimination would seem closely related to administrative discrimination discussed earlier.

V. INTERPROVINCIAL DIFFERENCES IN RISK

Even though banks are unlikely to actively discriminate among the various provinces, if a province is characterized by a high concentration of borrowers with poor risk characteristics, then one might expect banks to lend less and at higher rates than elsewhere. Thus as banks go about structuring their nationwide portfolio in an optimal way on the basis of the non-discriminatory application of general lending criteria to all classes of borrowers, their lending could exhibit an identifiable provincial and regional pattern. Quite apart from explicit discrimination this possibility could be a source of concern to provinces which would like to see a vigorous expansion of businesses which banks regard as high in risk.

Certainly concern over the possible regional effects of chartered bank lending policies has been the principal factor behind federal government efforts to influence the cost and availability of credit to slow-growth regions during periods of tight monetary policy. The Department of Finance noted in its brief at the Western Economic Opportunities Conference:

> "In periods when bank credit has had to be rationed, the central bank and the Minister of Finance have asked the chartered banks to have special regard for borrowers in slow-growth areas and for small businesses generally. The chartered banks have given assurances that they do pay special attention to the demands of small business and the needs of slow-growth areas. The emergence of dual-rate lending is indicative of developing policies in this regard."[11]

No attempt will be made in this study to define and test interprovincial differences in financial risk or to examine the loan portfolios of banks to see if the provincial allocation of their portfolios is consistent with what one might expect in the light of such risk differences. It, therefore, remains simply an interesting potential area of research as far as this study is concerned. That quantifiable risk differences do exist was implied by representatives of some major mortgage lenders interviewed during the course of this study. It was stated that major lenders attempt to evaluate mortgage risk when establishing mortgage rates in a given region by examining, when available, such data as: the level and fluctuations in personal per capita income, age/sex composition of the population, incidence of strikes, magnitude of fluctuations in unemployment and general business conditions, degree of industrial and economic diversification and household debt data.

VI. SUMMARY AND CONCLUSIONS

The major thrust of the analysis presented in this chapter is that geographical discrimination by banks is unlikely to be significant or persistent. This skepticism reflects several considerations which mitigate against the possibility of discrimination. These were seen to include such factors as the need for banks to retain the goodwill of their customers and the need as nationwide organizations to adopt standardized policies and procedures and criteria when vetting loan applications. Fundamentally, the question concerns the degree of integration of the Canadian banking and financial system. Since a high degree of integration and thus mobility of funds does exist, banks are unlikely to treat customers in one geographic area less favourably than in others.

Notes

[1]Economic Council of Canada, *Efficiency and Regulation,* pp. 12-14.

[2]Royal Commission on Banking and Finance, *Final Report,* 1964, p. 132.

[3]See, for example, the discussion in Chapter one of this monograph.

[4]The Canadian Bankers' Association, *The Industry's Brief,* Number 2 in a series, Bank Act 77, October, 1975.

[5]We are treating both the price and non-price terms and conditions on loans as though as they both affect the size of loan demanded by making loans more or less attractive (costly). To facilitate the following exposition, when interest rates are mentioned it is assumed that the discussion implicitly refers to non-interest rate terms as well.

[6]For a brief discussion of the concept of integration as it can be applied to capital markets, see T. Scitovsky, "The Theory of the Balance of Payments and the Problem of a Common European Currency," *Kyklos,* Vol. X, 1957, pp. 24-30.

[7]This statement refers, of course, to interest rate differences which exceed those which may exist should risk differences between bank borrowers in different locations exist. For the rest of this section, unless explicitly stated to the contrary, references to levels or differences in interest rates are made on the assumption that no risk differences exist.

[8]The Canadian Bankers' Association, *The Banks and the West,* July 1973, p. 10.

[9]*Mortgage News Letter,* issued monthly by the Mortgage Insurance Company of Canada, August 1972-July 1976.

[10]Jaffee, D.M., and Modigliani, F., "A Theory and Test of Credit Rationing," *American Economic Review,* 1969, pp. 850-872.

[11]Government of Canada, *Capital Financing and Financial Institutions,* p. 48.

Chapter III

The Banks and British Columbia:
Tests for Discrimination

Chapter III

The Banks and British Columbia: Tests for Discrimination

I. INTRODUCTION

This chapter examines selected banking and economic statistics for British Columbia and the rest of Canada to test for evidence of discrimination by the banks. Although the previous chapter suggests that discrimination is unlikely to exist in Canada, our confidence in that conclusion would be enhanced if a careful examination of available data provided corroborating evidence. The basic theme of the chapter is that properly conceived, the analysis of the provincial distribution of bank assets and liabilities is a problem in interregional trade and finance. In addition to acting as financial intermediaries banks also act as payments institutions. Thus, their provincial balance sheets reflect provincial current and capital account transactions. The debate over provincial banks has placed insufficient emphasis on the involvement of the banks as payments institutions in interprovincial financial relations.

The chapter begins with a review of the 'balance sheet test' for the existence of discrimination emphasizing the reasons why this test must be applied carefully and could be invalid. This discussion serves as the stepping stone to two alternative tests for discrimination: the flow of funds test and the money supply test. These two tests reveal that the data is consistent with the view that there has been no significant discrimination over the time periods concerned.

Finally, a brief review of British Columbia's economy is made for the period when discrimination was being alleged to provide a general view of whether the banks appear to be doing their job.

II. THE BALANCE SHEET TEST

One of the major sources of controversy in the debate over the need for provincial banks involves the role of banks as conduits whereby deposits are siphoned from one region for use in another. Deposits are sources of funds. Loans are uses of funds. As documented in Chapter I, some provinces have inferred from this that if deposits exceed loans in a particular province or region then banks must be discriminating against such areas. The analysis of the previous chapter seems, superficially, to support this view. If banks successfully implement administrative, interest rate, or credit rationing discrimination against borrowers in a province, the dollar amount of loans outstanding would be less than it would be in the absence of discrimination. By constructing a consolidated balance sheet for all bank branches in the region or province, data on total deposits and loans could be obtained and, depending upon whether deposits exceed or are smaller than loans, discrimination would seem to be proved or disproved, respectively.

Difficulties with simple test

There are several problems with this interpretation of bank branch data which can be classified as either statistical or analytical. On the statistical side, obstacles arise because of the deposit and loan booking activities of bank clients and the fact that banks' cash and liquid asset holdings are run on a centralized Canada-wide basis. A good example of the loan booking problem is the handling of grain loans. At the end of the first calendar quarter of 1975 bank loans to grain dealers amounted to about $1,500 million. Most were held on the books of the main branches of banks in Winnipeg, the administrative centre of the grain trade. But the loans represent credits to the grain business in each of the three prairie provinces, not just in Manitoba. Properly, they should appear on the asset side of the consolidated balance sheets of banks for each of those provinces.

Similar difficulties arise with respect to loans booked by national corporations in provinces other than the province in which the proceeds of the loans are spent. On the liability side of the balance sheet, problems are presented by federal government deposits which appear on the books of Ottawa bank branches, but which arise from the activities of the government in all provinces and regions of the country. Cash receipts of national corporations like Air Canada may be managed by their head office in Montreal and could result in a term deposit there when, in a sense, the deposits are generated by offices of Air Canada across the country. To paraphrase one banker: nothing much is proved about how banks allocate deposits by looking at the simple location of deposits and large business loans.[1]

Further difficulties are posed by the need for banks to hold cash and liquid asset reserves against their deposit liabilities. Banking system holdings of deposits at the Bank of Canada, Government of Canada Treasury bills and day-to-day loans are held on the books of the head office. But the need to hold reserves arises from the existence of deposits on the books of all of their branches in all regions of Canada. Thus, any attempt to identify how banks use a province's deposits must recognize that a certain proportion of such deposits must be held in the form of reserves at head office.

Adjustments necessary

Thus when the Canadian Bankers' Association decided to react to provincial allegations of discrimination it did not simply add up all of the deposits and loans on the books of branches in each of the provinces. Instead, it constructed complete balance sheets modifying the branch data for each province on the basis of arbitrary but necessary allocations of those special assets and liabilities which should be distributed to provinces other than those in which they may naturally be booked.[2] A statistically preferred test for discrimination is, therefore, a comparison of total adjusted provincial liabilities and assets, not a comparison of deposits and loans on the books of branches in each province.

Discrimination by depositors

The analytical problems associated with using a simple comparison of assets and liabilities as a test for discrimination arise because the geographic distribution of deposits is affected by deposit transfers initiated by the holders of bank deposits. Chequable bank deposits are, of course, the major means of payment in Canada. Purchases of goods, services and financial instruments by deposit holders give rise to deposit transfers within and between provinces. For example, suppose residents of a province, say British Columbia, write cheques on their branches in favour of a person in another province, say Ontario. As the cheques are deposited in Ontario branches of a bank, deposits in Ontario rise. After the cheques have been transferred back to British Columbia, deposits in British Columbia will have fallen. In British Columbia, liabilities of the banking system will have fallen relative to assets held in branches there, while in Ontario liabilities will have risen relative to assets. The involvement of the banks is passive. They execute the instructions of the drawer of the transfer but do not themselves initiate the deposit movement.

It should also be noted that because chartered banks balance their books on a national basis such interprovincial transfers do not necessarily give rise to other balance sheet adjustments. A bank operates on the basis of consolidated balance sheets across all branches and head office. Thus head office holds on its own books Bank of Canada deposits and other liquid asset reserves required by law against deposits held in branches across the country. For Canada as a whole, then, bank assets equal bank liabilities. But they are not required to balance their books regionally, or provincially, or by branch. Another implication is that the ability of any one branch to make loans does not depend on its own cash holdings but rather those arising from the activities of all branches and head office. It is up to the senior management of a bank to coordinate the operations of the branches and head office so that in aggregate, the bank meets legal and working liquidity requirements. Thus, remedial balance sheet adjustments are only required when net inter-bank transfers of deposits occur. Whether the transfer is between bank branches in one province or between bank branches in different provinces is irrelevant.

Clearly movements of provincial deposits will be related to the size and pattern of interprovincial and international trade and financial flows. If the value of incoming transfers to a province exceeds the value of outgoing transfers, deposits in that province will tend to rise and vice versa. The important implication for the interpretation of bank balance sheets is that the provincial distribution of bank deposits is largely outside the ability of the banks to control. Hence, if bank liabilities exceed assets in a particular province this cannot necessarily be interpreted as evidence of discrimination.

Table 1 shows banking system total assets and liabilities for British Columbia on an end of quarter basis between 1974 and 1976. On average, over the years as a whole assets exceeded liabilities by $540 million. If the balance sheet test were applied it would be concluded that British Columbia

TABLE 1
Total Bank Assets and Liabilities: British Columbia
By Quarters, 1974-1976

	Quarter	Assets ($ millions)	Liabilities ($ millions)	Net ($ millions)
1974	I	7,451	7,171	280
	II	7,880	7,607	273
	III	8,234	8,298	−64
	IV	8,656	8,471	185
Average		8,055	7,887	168
1975	I	8,929	8,454	475
	II	9,359	8,981	378
	III	9,668	9,030	638
	IV	10,025	9,214	811
Average		9,495	8,920	575
1976	I	10,364	9,323	1,041
	II	11,163	10,090	1,073
	III	11,643	10,951	692
	IV	11,947	11,242	705
Average		11,279	10,402	877

Source: *Bank of Canada Review*, Selected Issues, 1975-1977, Tables 12 and 13.

was not discriminated against by the banks. Similarly, strict application of the test would indicate that during 1974, discrimination was evident in the third quarter. Obviously this borders on the ridiculous. The simple comparison of asset and liability data does not constitute an adequate test of discrimination. Thus, the regional balance sheet data offered by the Canadian Bankers' Association in rebuttal to provincial allegations of discrimination do not prove that discrimination does not exist. At the same time they are not inconsistent with the view that discrimination does not exist.

III. BANKING STATISTICS AND INTERPROVINCIAL TRADE AND CAPITAL FLOWS

If there is no simple relationship between bank liabilities and assets (or deposits and loans) what does determine their provincial distribution? The implication of the description of the nature of bank operations both as payments institutions and financial intermediaries, is that the location of those liabilities and assets which are held at the branch level should reflect interprovincial trade and financial relationships. To test this implication the structure of British Columbia's balance of payments was examined.

The structure of the British Columbia economy

In a 1971 paper, R.A. Shearer noted that, on the basis of 1961 statistics, British Columbia was:

> "an economy relatively heavily specialized in natural resource extraction and processing, with little true secondary manufacturing but. . .with a very large service sector."[3]

Although these statistics related to British Columbia more than fifteen years ago, Shearer also examined data between 1961 and 1966 and found little that would indicate a basic change in the structure of the economy:

> "The economic expansion in British Columbia in 1961-1966. . .was quite narrowly focused on the further development of native-natural-resource extraction and

processing facilities (including hydro-electric power). Some of the expansion has been relatively very capital-intensive...The service sector has continued to expand...but there is little evidence of a major upsurge in secondary manufacturing which is not tied directly to the processing of native-natural-resources...The expanding economic base remains much as it always has been: the exploitation of mineral and forest resources (with tourism and recreation increasing in importance)."[4]

Employment statistics published by the Department of Economic Development of the Government of British Columbia suggest that in the years from 1967 to 1974 the structure of the British Columbia economy continued to follow historical patterns. Employment in forest products and mineral products industries rose by 14 per cent and 39 per cent respectively over the years concerned while employment in the service sector has outpaced that of other industries by sizable amounts, rising 43 per cent over the same period. Manufacturing and construction employment grew as well, but less rapidly than in the primary or service sectors.

Additional evidence as to the stability of the province's natural resource base is provided by statistics on the province's goods producing industries. The value of primary forestry and mining production rose from 18.1 per cent of industry total in 1967 to 20 per cent in 1974. In fact, as Table 2 suggests, the non agricultural based resource industries have become increasingly important while manufacturing and construction's combined share of industry output has declined. This pattern is not too different from that of Canada as a whole, which has seen the overall contribution of primary production rise by about 3 percentage points, from 26 to 29 per cent of total production over the years 1967 to 1974.

TABLE 2
Census Value Added in Goods
Producing Industries
1967 and 1974
(Industry percentages of total)

| | 1967 | | 1974 | |
	B.C.	Canada	B.C.	Canada
Agriculture	4.3	9.0	3.0	9.0
Forestry	10.2	2.3	8.5	1.9
Fisheries	1.6	0.6	1.5	0.4
Trapping	—	—	—	—
Mining	7.9	9.8	11.5	13.5
Electric Power	4.5	4.1	4.4	4.1
Manufacturing	45.9	57.0	47.7	53.1
Construction	25.6	17.2	23.4	18.0

Source: Statistics Canada, *Survey of Production,* Annual, 1967 and 1974, Catalogue number 61-202.

British Columbia's balance of trade

No detailed statistics are regularly compiled on provincial exports and imports of goods and services. However, recent federal estimates of the major components of gross provincial product for the 1961-1974 period indicate that British Columbia has consistently had (with the exception of 1973) a current account deficit *vis à vis* the rest of the world.[5] However, since the balance on current account was calculated as a residual, separate estimates of export and import levels are not available.

Commodity trade estimates have been reported by R.A. Shearer for the early 1960s.[6] They provide some insight into the nature of the province's trade. Total exports of commodities exceeded total imports during the years 1961-1964. Exports were dominated by forest products and minerals while about 80 per cent of exports were sold to foreign countries with 20 per cent going to other provinces in Canada. Imports consisted mainly of consumer goods, machinery and equipment and construction materials, about 70 per cent of them being bought from the rest of Canada. As Shearer notes, these estimates suggest that British Columbia was running a deficit in its balance of trade with the rest of Canada and a surplus with foreign countries. On balance its merchandise exports exceed its imports resulting in a surplus on commodity trade.

Some further evidence regarding British Columbia's trade may be gained from total Canadian export data. Over the 1967 to 1974 period Canadian exports of forest products rose by over 140 per cent while mineral and metal exports jumped over 200 per cent. This growth exceeded that of Canadian gross national product which increased 110 per cent during these years. Since forest products and minerals play such a large role in total commodity exports from British Columbia the province must have enjoyed rapid growth in its exports as well.

However, as Shearer stresses, if estimates of exports and imports of services had been available, British Columbia's current account deficit *vis à vis* the rest of Canada would probably have been larger. Given that the Statistics Canada estimates yield an overall trade deficit, we can infer that the balance of trade related to services is indeed substantial enough to offset entirely the commodity trade surplus generated by exports to foreign countries.

British Columbia's capital accounts

No statistics are collected on the province's financial relationships with the rest of Canada or the world. Although estimates of investment spending are available, there are no estimates of gross provincial savings. However, it seems likely that British Columbia has been a net importer of long-term savings from the rest of the world—from both domestic and foreign sources. Shearer has previously argued that:

> "Cumulative capital expenditures in British Columbia in the period 1948-66 amounted to about 12 per cent of total capital expenditures in Canada. We have no information on gross provincial savings. However, over the same period personal income in British Columbia averaged about 10 per cent of that in Canada as a whole. Provincial gross income probably varied roughly in proportion to personal income, and it is reasonable to assume that savings did also. Coupled with the fact that

Canada as a whole was not a capital importer in this period, this suggests that British Columbia must have been a net capital importer. What was true of 1948-66 must have been even more so for earlier periods."[7]

There is no reason to suppose that the structure of the British Columbia economy has changed sufficiently to warrant a revision of this view for the period 1967 to 1974.

British Columbia's deposits, loans and balance of payments

Although the statistical picture of British Columbia's trade and capital relationships with the rest of the world has been sketchy, it does have certain implications for the province's banking data. It has been pointed out that nationwide banks do not have to balance their assets and liabilities on a provincial basis. However, the deposits and loans recorded in a particular province by the banks probably reflect the structure of its economy and the nature of its balance of payments with the other provinces and with foreign countries.

As mentioned earlier, comprehensive data on the provincial assets and liabilities of the chartered banks has been published since 1974 by the Bank of Canada.[8] They show that during 1976, of total Canadian bank assets, 13.2 per cent may be reasonably allocated to British Columbia. The selected asset data shown in Table 3 offer some indication of the composition of bank assets in British Columbia and the rest of Canada. In 1976, British Columbia bank assets were more heavily concentrated in mortgages insured under the National Housing Act and business loans than in the rest of Canada, much more heavily concentrated in other residential mortgages and personal loans, and less heavily devoted to farm loans. Unfortunately, no industry breakdown of business loans is available. A comparison of the proportion of British Columbia assets to total Canadian bank assets (including British Columbia) reveals that the banks make 25 per cent of their other (non-insured) residential mortgages in British Columbia.[9]

TABLE 3
Chartered Bank Asset Composition
British Columbia and the Rest of Canada[1]
Average of Quarterly Data, 1976

Selected Assets	B.C.		Rest of Canada		B.C. share of total Canada (%)[3]
	$ millions	% of total assets	$ millions	% of total assets[2]	
Mortgages (N.H.A. insured)	716	6.3	3,989	5.4	15.2
Other residential mortgages	918	8.1	2,740	3.7	25.1
Total personal loans	2,582	22.9	13,598	18.4	16.0
Total business loans	3,620	32.1	22,900	30.9	13.6
Farm loans	222	2.0	2,802	3.8	7.3
Total Assets	11,279		74,036		13.2

[1]Excluding head office and/or international totals and British Columbia.
[2]Will not sum to total assets as several asset types omitted. The latter include assets held at head office which can only be arbitrarily assigned to a specific province such as Government of Canada securities.
[3]Including British Columbia.
Source: *Bank of Canada Review*, October 1976 and July 1977, Table 12.

On the liability side of the balance sheet, it can be seen from Table 4 that during 1976 British Columbia accounted for about 13 per cent of total Canadian liabilities. The composition of deposits is most heavily concentrated in personal savings deposits with about the same proportion of demand deposits and relatively less deposits of the non-personal notice type than the rest of Canada. The latter probably reflects centralization of cash management by British Columbia corporations and the placement of this cash in Eastern money market centres. This is consistent with the Economic Council data on the location of bank deposits reported earlier.

Deficits and deposits

The discussion of British Columbia's economy and balance of payments suggested that British Columbia has a net deficit on current account. It has a trade deficit with the rest of Canada which is accentuated by an overall deficit on services account. Statistics Canada estimates mentioned above show British Columbia as having an overall current account deficit. Thus, we conclude that the export surplus that British Columbia has with the rest of the world must be more than offset by the services deficit. Previous discussion also suggests that British Columbia is likely a net importer of long-term capital from the rest of the world, including Canada.

The size of total bank liabilities will be affected by the magnitude of the province's net current account and long-term capital flows since these transactions will generally be carried out using chartered bank deposits. A current account deficit means that British Columbia residents are receiving less from outside the province than they are paying out of the province for goods and services. If the net long-term capital inflow is less than, equal to, or larger than the current account deficit chartered bank deposits in British Columbia will tend to fall, remain the same, or rise, respectively. In this way, the deposit accounts of the chartered banks automatically and passively tend to reflect the underlying trends in the province's balance of payments. Any persistent tendency for British Columbia's deposits to fall would tend to

TABLE 4

Chartered Bank Deposit Composition British Columbia and the Rest of Canada

Average of Quarterly Data, 1976[1]

Selected Deposits	B.C.		Rest of Canada		B.C. Share of Total for Canada (%)
	$millions	& of total liabilities[2]	$ millions	% of total liabilities[2]	
Total personal savings	5,212	50.1	32,947	47.4	13.7
Total other notice	1,668	16.0	14,830	21.3	10.1
Total other demand	1,692	16.3	11,179	16.1	13.1
Total	8,572				
Total Liabilities	10,402		69,514		13.0

[1]Excludes head office and/or international and British Columbia.

[2]Will not sum to total liabilities as several categories of deposit and liability are omitted. The latter include such items as Government of Canada deposits and accumulated appropriations for losses which can only be arbitrarily assigned to a specific province.

Source: *Bank of Canada Review*, October 1976 and July 1977, Table 13.

reduce total chartered bank liabilities in the province below total banking system holdings of provincial assets.[10]

Referring to Tables 3 and 4 again, we can compare total chartered bank assets, largely loans, and total chartered bank liabilities, largely deposits, which have been attributed to British Columbia by the Bank of Canada. These figures for total assets and liabilities include a number of account categories quite apart from the few selected loan and deposit items mentioned in the previous section. The Tables show that on average during 1976 total chartered bank assets for British Columbia exceeded total liabilities by about $0.9 billion. On balance, then, chartered bank assets exceed liabilities in the province by a fairly sizeable amount. This suggests that British Columbia's net long-term capital inflows are smaller than the province's current account deficit. This would lead to a tendency for the province's deposits to be lower than would otherwise be the case, thereby holding down total liabilities. [11]

Chartered bank balance sheet data is, therefore, consistent with a certain picture, described above, of British Columbia's trade and financial relationships with the rest of the world, including the rest of Canada. There is no evidence of discrimination in the sense that British Columbia's banking data is incompatible with what one might have expected on the basis of available information on the structure of the province's balance of payments.

It is recognized that there is a stock/flow problem in making this sort of inference. Balance of payments accounts measure flows while banking balance sheet data measure stocks. However, to the extent that British Columbia's balance of payments has displayed a similar pattern for many years, the banking data may be regarded as the cumulative result of the province's trade and financial relationships.

It has been suggested earlier that it seems likely that British Columbia has been experiencing similar patterns in its trade and capital relationships for years. It would have been interesting to have had access to detailed balance of payments accounts which would have permitted a more intensive examination of these relationships and their implications for the province's banking data. Such data is not available. Nor do published provincial banking statistics extend back for many years. As noted previously, actual Canadian dollar deposit data is not reported prior to 1974. On the other hand, selected loan data are reported by the Bank of Canada by quarter from the end of the first quarter of 1972.[12] However, the latter include only business loans of less than $100,000 and thus would give little idea of the total value of loans attributed to the province.

The money supply test

Using a little ingenuity it is nevertheless possible to construct a Canadian dollar deposit series for British Columbia and compare it to Canadian dollar deposits for the rest of Canada for the years 1968 through 1974. Such a series provides indirect evidence on the existence of discrimination.

One of the aspects of discrimination mentioned in Chapter II involved banks offering less attractive deposit rates and service charges to customers in a particular province, say, British Columbia. This by itself would retard the growth of bank deposits in that province compared to others. The province would receive less of the national money supply than would otherwise be the case. It has been argued above that British Columbia's balance of trade is probably giving rise to a net outflow of deposits. These considerations together suggest that if there is indeed discrimination against banking customers in British Columbia, the growth of deposits in the province would be below the national average and that the share of the total money supply would be low by comparison with the province's share in economic activity.

Table 5 presents the time series of banking system private Canadian dollar deposits for British Columbia and the rest of Canada as at April 30 for the years 1968 to 1976. It can be seen that deposits in the province have averaged in size about 12 to 12.5 per cent of the total of deposits held by other provinces in Canada. It is estimated that British Columbia's deposits grew at an annual rate in excess of 15 per cent over the years 1968 to 1976. The slowdown in 1970 may reflect the tight monetary policy being pursued during the

TABLE 5
Canadian Dollar Deposits of Chartered Banks
1968-1976
($ millions)

	British Columbia		All of Canada		British Columbia/ All of Canada (per cent)
	Amount	Per cent Change	Amount	Per cent Change	
1968	2,545		21,936		11.6
1969	3,036	19.3	24,889	13.5	12.2
1970	3,204	5.5	25,632	3.0	12.5
1971	3,703	15.6	29,159	13.8	12.7
1972	4,176	12.8	34,509	18.3	12.1
1973	4,758	13.9	39,324	13.9	12.1
1974	6,001	26.1	46,217	17.5	13.0
1975	6,832	13.8	54,691	18.3	12.5
1976	7,754	13.5	62,655	14.6	12.4
Average		15.1		14.1	12.3

Source: 1968 to 1972 statistics are based on a table on p. 8 of a publication of the Canadian Bankers' Association entitled *The Banks and the West,* a special edition of the C.B.A. Bulletin, Volume 16, No. 2, July 1973. April 30 deposit levels for the whole of Canada were calculated excluding federal, provincial governments and other banks using end of period statistics published by the Bank of Canada (See Table 8, September, 1975, *Bank of Canada Review).* British Columbia deposit shares reported in *The Banks and the West* were applied to the Canadian totals. For 1973 the British Columbia deposit figure was obtained by applying the Canada total deposit growth rate of 13.95%. For 1974 on, the end of first quarter Canadian dollar deposit total excluding federal and provincial governments and other banks was obtained from Table 13, *Bank of Canada Review,* Selected Issues, 1975 to 1977.

1969 to 1970 anti-inflation programme of the federal government. Even so, British Columbia's deposits grew more rapidly in that year than those of the rest of Canada which recorded an increase of only 3 per cent.

Accordingly, there is no evidence from relative growth rates of the money supply to support the contention of consistent discrimination.

Another test for discrimination can be made by evaluating whether British Columbia's share of the money supply is in keeping with the province's share of national economic activity. Table 6 presents data on the province's gross provincial product and Canadian gross national product. Over the years 1968 to 1976, British Columbia's output grew on average by 12.3 per cent compared to 11.3 per cent for the rest of Canada. This more rapid growth rate for the province was reflected in an increase in the share of national output

TABLE 6
British Columbia Gross Provincial Product
and Canadian Gross National Product,
1968-1975

| | British Columbia | | Rest of Canada[1] | | B.C.'s Share of Total Canadian GNP in % |
	$ millions (1)	% change (2)	$ millions (3)	% change (4)	
1968	7,814		64,772		10.8
1969	8,869	13.5	70,946	5.4	11.1
1970	9,463	6.7	76,222	7.4	11.0
1971	10,610	12.1	83,505	9.6	11.3
1972	11,919	12.3	92,750	11.1	11.4
1973	14,088	18.2	108,494	17.0	11.5
1974	16,685	18.4	127,931	17.9	11.6
1975	18,357	10.0	142,775	11.6	11.4
Average		13.0		11.4	

[1]Canadian GNP less British Columbia GPP.
Sources: Department of Economic Development, Government of British Columbia, *British Columbia Summary of Economic Activity, 1974, 1975*, Statistical Supplement.
Department of Finance, *Economic Review*, May 1977, p. 125.

from 10.8 per cent to 11.5 per cent. Thus, the province's share of the national supply of bank money is about one percentage point higher than its share of total output. On this basis, it seems that British Columbia's stock of bank deposits is reasonable, and that there is no evidence on discrimination from this source.

It is a moot question as to whether or not the province's relatively larger share of the money supply was a major source of the more rapid rate of growth in total output.[13] Other factors certainly played a part. During the years 1968 to 1976 gross investment spending in British Columbia increased on average by 14.2 per cent compared to 12.2 per cent for the rest of Canada.[14] These were also years of strong export sales for British Columbia. Finally, British Columbia experienced extraordinary growth in labour force and population—more than double the Canadian rate—at 3 and 4.8 per cent respectively.[15] British Columbia's strong economic performance is also captured by employment data which show that employment grew in the province on average 4.7 per cent over the years 1967 to 1974 compared to 2.9 per cent for the other provinces.[16]

73

IV. SUMMARY AND CONCLUSIONS

The objective of this chapter was to attempt to determine statistically the existence or absence of discrimination. In the light of the quality of available data on the British Columbia economy and financial system this turned out to be a rather heroic task. If nothing else, the chapter is evidence of the great need for improved trade and financial statistics, on a provincial basis, so that the operation of provincial economies and their inter-relationships can be better understood. Be that as it may, the chapter did demonstrate that the balance sheet approach to discrimination so visible in the debate over provincial banks has many pitfalls. In short, a simple comparison of deposits and loans is not a valid test of discrimination. At the same time, the total liabilities and assets approach followed by the banks serves to obfuscate the role of the banks in the economy. The provincial distribution of bank deposits and loans is not mystical or a matter of conspiracy. It is the natural consequence of funds in Canada moving in response to economic incentives and payments activities of the public.

There is great irony in the debate over the impact of banks on provincial holdings of deposits and loans. In order for banks to ensure that deposits and loans (or liabilities and assets) are balanced between provinces they would be forced to institute interprovincial differences in administrative procedures, prices and credit standards. That is, a prerequisite to provincially-balanced books is effective discrimination. In Canada today, such discrimination would be directed mainly against Ontario. But this is impossible in a sophisticated, highly-integrated, common currency system. Thus (in the absence of any sound economic or legal reasons why bank books should balance provincially) the existence in Canada of provincial differences between bank loans and deposits is evidence that banks are doing their job in a non-discriminatory manner.

Acceptance of the view that chartered bank discrimination is not a valid cause for concern in the debate over provincial ownership of banks does not constitute a rejection of the need for provincial government banks. Even in the absence of discrimination provincial governments can be legitimately concerned about inadequacies which they perceive in the operations of chartered banks which hinder the achievement of provincial economic and social goals. The next chapter tackles the question of whether the other concerns of provincial governments constitute sufficient grounds to warrant establishment of provincial public banks.

Notes

[1] R.M. MacIntosh, "National Banks and Regional Interest," address to The Canadian Club, Winnipeg, Manitoba, April 5, 1973.

[2] Recently the Bank of Canada has begun to publish a regional distribution (provincial, Yukon, Territories, Head Office, and/or International) of bank assets and liabilities. The assumptions which are required to construct these accounts can be found in notes to Tables 12 and 13 of the *Bank of Canada Review.*

[3] R. Shearer, "The Economy of British Columbia," in R. Shearer, J. Young and G. Munro, *Trade Liberalization and Regional Economy: Studies of the Impact of Free Trade in British Columbia,* University of Toronto Press, Toronto, 1971, p. 11.

[4] *Ibid.,* p. 25.

[5] These estimates were recently published by Statistics Canada. See, Statistics Canada, Gross National Product Division, *Provincial Economic Accounts 1961-1974,* Experimental Data, Table 2.

[6] R.A. Shearer, *op. cit.*

[7] *Ibid.,* footnote 61, p. 33.

[8] See *Bank of Canada Review,* June, 1977, Tables 12 and 13. This end of quarter data series begins with the first quarter of 1974. Prior to that date statistics had been compiled by the Canadian Bankers' Association on the provincial allocation of total Canadian liabilities and assets as at October 31, 1972 and presented to the participants of the Western Economic Opportunities Conference in July 1973. Quarterly provincial data on certain selected bank assets has been published since November 1972 in the monthly *Bank of Canada Review.*

[9] The possibility that British Columbia has been an important recipient of mortgage funds in Canada receives some additional support from statistics published by the Central Mortgage and Housing Corporation. They show that an increase from 12 per cent in 1968 to 14 per cent in 1976 in the province's participation in total N.H.A. and conventional mortgage loans approved by lending institutions, by dwelling units. C.M.H.C., *Canadian Housing Statistics,* 1976, Table 46, p. 40.

[10]I am indebted to Dr. J.A. Galbraith, Chief Economist, Sun Life Assurance Company of Canada, for assistance in explaining this point. Any remaining lack of clarity is the responsibility of the author alone.

[11]It is not possible to offer some explanations for the anomalous provincial banking statistics reported for the third quarter of 1974 shown in Table 1 above which was pointed out earlier. A careful examination of Bank of Canada statistics reveals that there was a substantial surge in deposits in that quarter which swamped a simultaneous but smaller increase in loans. It is relevant to speculate on the source of that deposit surge in the light of the discussion of the province's balance of payments. Was it due to a seasonal inflow of export receipts? Was there an unusually large bond sale by the province to the rest of the world? Did the borrowers from banks use their funds primarily within the province rather than for importing goods? Was there a large shift in deposits from other provincial banking type institutions to the banks? Each of these questions embodies a legitimate possibility. Together they are indicative of how complex the determinants of the behaviour of deposits and loans are.

[12]The categories of selected loans are ordinary personal loans, farm loans, business loans under authorized limits of less than $100,000, loans to provinces and municipalities, provincial and municipal securities, mortgages insured under N.H.A. and other residential mortgages.

[13]Regardless of the answer, provincial credit unions were participating in the province's growth as well. As part of the statistical research for this study an attempt was made to collect information for several years on the liabilities and assets of near banks operating in British Columbia. Only credit unions' statistics were obtained. A summary of this data is presented in the Appendix to this chapter in the expectation that it will be of interest to readers of this study.

[14]Statistics Canada, *Public and Private Investment in Canada,* 1969-1977, Catalogue No. 61-205, annual.

[15]Central Mortgage and Housing Corporation, *Canadian Housing Statistics,* 1974. *Bank of Canada Review,* September 1975, Tables 56 and 57.

[16]*Bank of Canada Review,* September, 1975.

Appendix

British Columbia Credit Unions

By the end of 1975 British Columbia credit unions, excluding the British Columbia central, held assets amounting to 15.5 per cent of the banking system's total assets in the province. The structure of the assets of the credit unions reveals several interesting features. Appendix Table A-1 shows that cash and demand deposits held were a strikingly low proportion of total assets—about 3 to 4 per cent since 1969. This contrasts sharply with the 11 to 12 per cent cash and demand deposits held by credit unions in the whole of Canada. British Columbia credit union assets have become heavily concentrated in mortgage loans. Since 1967 the share of mortgage loans in their portfolio has almost doubled. By the end of 1975, two-thirds of their total assets were in mortgage loans while only 14.4 per cent were devoted to personal loans. The rest of the assets are relatively insignificant by comparison.

This also contrasts with portfolio composition of credit unions on a Canada-wide basis.[1] In the latter, personal loans have made up about 30 per cent of total Canadian assets over the nine years shown. Since 1970 they have gradually declined as a per cent of total assets (to 27 per cent in 1975), but much less dramatically than for British Columbia. Mortgage loans have increased from about 30 per cent of assets in 1967-1971 to 39 per cent in 1975. Even after this recent spurt

---

[1]Because the Canada data reported in Appendix Table A-1 includes data for British Columbia the differences being pinpointed would be even greater had the British Columbia credit unions been excluded.

APPENDIX TABLE A-1

Credit Union Selected Assets, Per cent of Total

British Columbia and Canada (including B.C.)[1]

End of Year, 1967-1975

(in per cent)

	Cash and Demand Deposits		Term Deposits		Investments in all Governments		Personal Loans		Farm Loans		Mortgage Loans	
	B.C.	Canada	B.C.	Canada	B.C.	Canada	B.C.	Canada	B.C.	Canada	B.C.	Canada
1967	4.8	11.0	4.3	3.0	0.8	12.0	43.9	32.3	0.8	2.5	37.1	28.8
1968	9.1	11.1	0.9	2.6	0.8	10.8	41.6	32.6	0.6	2.3	38.8	30.0
1969	2.7	10.6	6.1	3.5	0.8	10.9	37.7	33.0	1.6	2.5	42.9	29.8
1970	3.2	11.8	6.2	3.6	1.0	11.4	37.0	32.5	0.5	2.1	43.8	29.1
1971	3.6	13.0	7.1	4.0	1.0	12.9	28.2	30.1	0.4	2.1	51.7	29.9
1972	2.9	12.3	6.5	4.7	1.3	11.4	21.3	29.0	0.2	1.2	61.5	32.9
1973	3.0	10.5	6.0	5.8	1.1	8.7	17.7	28.0	0.2	1.2	66.0	36.5
1974	3.8	12.9	5.2	5.6	0.5	7.7	16.2	27.7	0.2	1.2	67.3	39.0
1975	4.1	11.2	6.0	9.4	0.8	5.3	14.4	26.6	0.2	1.3	67.5	39.3

[1]Excludes centrals.

Source: Statistics Canada. *Credit Unions*, Annual. Catalogue No. 61-209, 1967-1975.

in mortgage loan growth the concentration of mortgage loans in all Canadian credit unions was less than 60 per cent of the concentration observed in credit unions in British Columbia.

This increasing emphasis on mortgages has been carried out during a period of extraordinary growth as Appendix Table A-2 shows. From 1971 to 1975 credit unions in the province have been increasing their assets at an average annual rate of 35 per cent. Over the 1967 to 1975 period they have experienced growth of just over 27 per cent per year compared to just under 17 per cent for credit unions in the rest of Canada. The consequence has been that the size of their total assets expressed as a percentage of the total assets of credit unions in the rest of Canada almost doubled between 1967 and 1975 (rising from 7.6 to 14.4 per cent).

The impressive growth performance of the British Columbia credit unions is evidence that provincially-based deposit-taking institutions behave in ways which differ significantly from nationwide institutions. It is clear that the growth of credit unions in British Columbia has far outpaced

APPENDIX TABLE A-2
Total Assets of Local Credit Unions[1]
British Columbia and Rest of Canada
End of Year, 1967-1975

	British Columbia		Rest of Canada		B.C. as a % of Rest of Canada
	($'000's)	% change	($'000's)	% change	
1967	236,576		3,131,156		7.6
1968	280,431	18.5	3,419,409	9.2	8.2
1969	317,612	13.3	3,746,444	9.6	8.5
1970	351,715	10.7	4,240,238	13.2	8.3
1971	478,162	36.0	5,109,566	20.5	9.4
1972	682,651	42.8	6,078,573	19.0	11.2
1973	992,634	45.4	7,473,152	22.9	13.3
1974	1,210,802	22.0	8,815,455	18.0	13.7
1975	1,554,269	28.4	10,777,110	22.3	14.4
Average 1968-1975		27.1		16.8	

[1]Excludes centrals.
Source: Statistics Canada, *Credit Unions*, Annual, 1967-1975, Catalogue number 61-209.

APPENDIX TABLE A-3
Credit Union Selected Liabilities, Per cent of Total
British Columbia and Canada (including B.C.)[1]
End of Year, 1967-1975
(per cent of total liabilities plus capital accounts)

	Accounts and Loans Payable[2]		Member Demand Deposits		Member Term Deposits[3]		Share Capital, Reserves and Undivided Surplus	
	B.C.	Canada	B.C.	Canada	B.C.	Canada	B.C.	Canada
1967	10.3	3.6	11.2	47.4	10.6	5.5	68.0	43.5
1968	11.4	3.5	14.1	46.4	14.6	3.8	59.9	42.5
1969	12.5	3.6	18.1	46.9	17.1	10.4	52.3	38.9
1970	8.4	2.6	21.7	49.4	22.6	14.3	47.3	33.6
1971	4.6	2.1	28.9	45.3	27.6	21.7	39.0	30.8
1972	6.5	2.9	32.1	45.1	30.0	23.3	31.4	28.1
1973	6.3	3.7	29.4	43.4	40.5	27.0	23.8	25.4
1974	8.5	4.4	27.2	43.8	45.5	28.8	18.8	23.0
1975	5.2	4.1	34.3	44.5	44.3	30.0	16.2	21.4

[1]Excludes centrals.
[2]Includes "Other Liabilities".
[3]Includes "Other Deposits".
Source: Statistics Canada. *Credit Unions*, Annual. Catalogue number 61-209, 1967-1975.

that of the banks in recent years. This must reflect success in attracting deposits from the banks and in keeping those deposits circulating in the credit union system once they are captured.

Appendix Table A-3 shows that the liabilities of British Columbia credit unions have become much more heavily concentrated in term deposits and demand deposits since 1967. There has been a corresponding decline in reliance placed on their capital accounts (share capital, reserves and undivided surplus) as a source of funds in their operations. This confirms the success of credit unions in British Columbia in competing away deposits from other institutions. In Canada as a whole a similar, but less rapidly increasing, reliance on deposit growth is apparent, although the mix of deposits is different. Demand deposits make up a greater proportion and term deposits a smaller proportion, of total liabilities than is the case in British Columbia.

Chapter IV

Economic Implications of Provincial Government Ownership of Banks

Chapter IV

Economic Implications of Provincial Government Ownership of Banks

I. INTRODUCTION

This chapter sets aside the issue of discrimination and extends the analysis of provincial government banking to include a consideration of the nature, size and distribution of the costs and benefits expected to flow from the intervention of a provincial bank in a province's retail banking business.[1] The term 'provincial bank' is used to describe a chartered bank owned and controlled by a provincial government. In contrast the term 'private bank' will be used to refer to chartered banks whose voting shares are wholly privately-owned.

On the basis of the review of the debate over provincial ownership of banks presented in Chapter I, it may be anticipated that a prime objective of the retail operations of a new provincial bank will be to offer credit to high risk borrowers under less stringent terms and conditions than such borrowers could obtain from private banks. Other goals would also be pursued. Important among them would be improving the balance between loans and deposits in local (especially rural and northern) communities, promoting greater retention of funds in the province, and providing greater competition to private banks with a view to reducing interest rates on private bank loans throughout the province.

The key issue

The key public policy issue provincial banking raises is that, although certain economic and social objectives of the government may be achieved, residents of the province and the provincial economy may have to pay for this success in the form of generally higher taxes and reduced economic well being. In short, social and economic costs as well as benefits may be anticipated. An informed decision on the desirability of a provincial bank requires judgements about the nature, size and distribution of the benefits and costs. Are the net benefits positive or negative? How do the net benefits change as the bank increases its market share? How are the benefits and costs distributed among the residents of the province?

Definitive judgements on the answers to such questions would require an exhaustive study where informed assumptions would be made about the probable structure, organization, size, efficiency, credit policies and objectives of a proposed provincial bank. This is beyond the scope of this chapter.[2] Instead our more modest intention is to offer insights into the types of questions which should be asked and the sorts of repercussions which should be anticipated when evaluating the need for a new provincial bank. Major economic impacts and implications are enumerated and analyzed in the hope that provincial government proposals can be evaluated in a more informed manner.

Understanding critical

The general theme of the chapter is that a provincial bank is not a costless remedy for the shortcomings provincial governments perceive in their provincial banking systems. Furthermore, the costs may be expected to rise sharply if provincial banks attempt to pursue credit policies which are misguided in terms of their understanding of the way the private banking system operates. The same competitive forces which mold the character of the operations of private banks across Canada will constrain the ability of a provincial bank to affect credit flows in the province and to confine the benefits and costs of its operations to residents of the province. On balance, it is difficult to be sanguine about the size of any net benefits which are expected to accrue to the province through the intervention of a full service provincial bank in the financial marketplace.

II. ISSUES IN THE ECONOMIC EFFECTS OF PROVINCIAL GOVERNMENT BANKING

The influence of a new provincial government bank on credit flows in a province emanates from management decisions regarding the types of deposit and loan markets in which the bank competes and the policies which govern the terms and conditions on which it is prepared to deal with lenders and borrowers. Management decisions must be consistent with the objectives and purposes of the provincial government. Provincial government control over those decisions and of bank policy generally arises from its ownership of the voting shares issued by the bank. That ownership enables the government to elect the board of directors and thereby monitor and regulate the activities of the executive officers and financial and corporate policies of the bank. Since they are government appointees it must be assumed that the board of directors will make decisions consistent with government policy.

A. The lower lending rate/higher tax nexus

The precise way in which a provincial bank interprets and implements government policies will be reflected in its pricing policies and in the quality and composition of the bank's capital accounts, liabilities, and assets. To simplify the analysis it is assumed that the government owns 100 per cent of the shares of the bank and that the funds used to purchase the shares are raised by the issue (or non-retirement) of government bonds. Thus, whether ownership of the bank, per se, worsens or improves the fiscal position of the government depends on whether it earns a rate of return on its bank shares less than or greater than the interest it pays on the bonds. If the former situation were to arise, then a reasonable implication is that the government must either raise taxes and/or issue new bonds to finance the deficit. In the case of a surplus, taxes could be reduced and/or bonds retired. If the rate of return on bank earnings equals the rate of interest on government bonds then the government 'breaks even'.

It should be noted that this criteria for evaluating the fiscal effects of a provincial bank is less demanding than some others. For example, if the provincial government switched pension funds out of private securities into its bank's shares, the required break even rate of return would probably be higher. Provincial governments typically pay a lower rate of interest on bonds than private bond issuers. Another alternative would be to finance the bank out of general tax revenues. In this case the cost takes the form of increased provincial taxes. This may be a price the public is willing to pay. Clearly several provincial governments have believed so in the past.

To reiterate, if a provincial bank does not earn enough on its assets to at least compensate the provincial government for the cost of equity funds, then insofar as its operations as a crown corporation are concerned it is a drain on government financial resources and a burden to the taxpayers of the province.

Profit policy

The profit policy of a provincial bank may be expected to be a low gross profit policy. For banks and other intermediaries before-tax profit may be viewed, in rough terms, as the difference between revenue earned (mainly interest on loans and other securities) and the sum total of the cost of funds (mainly interest on deposits) and intermediation costs. The latter include salaries, administrative expenses and other variable and fixed costs of the bank. In short, to make a gross profit the bank's interest receipts on loans and other securities must exceed intermediation and deposit costs. Since crown corporations do not have to pay corporate income tax, and provincial governments are unlikely to demand as high a rate of return as private shareholders, gross profits earned by the provincial bank expressed as a percentage of shareholders equity can be relatively low compared to private banks.

Revenue loss from lower interest rates?

This low profit policy would be carried out within the context of pricing policies on deposits and loans which also reflect the involvement of the government. The provincial government would likely encourage government agencies, departments, corporations and other institutions to place available funds on deposit at the bank. If the bank paid less interest on such deposits than the agencies, etc. could have earned at private banking or other financial institutions, general revenues of the government would fall. An opportunity cost is sustained. Given the level of government spending, tax levels or the size of outstanding debt would have to be higher. The rest of the bank's deposits would have to be attracted away from private banks in the markets for chequing and non-chequing deposits of households, businesses and other governments (especially municipal).

Provincial bank's interest advantage

Assuming that the provincial bank paid competitive interest rates on all of its deposits and that its intermediation costs were comparable to those of private institutions, then it would be in a good position to pursue its prime objective: lending to high risk customers and high risk regions and favouring them with lower interest rates than they would have had to pay for credit elsewhere, if they had been able to get it at all. The following simplified example gives some idea of the nature of the interest rate advantage a provincial bank might have over private banks. Assume:

1. the government originally issued $10 million in bonds bearing an annual coupon rate of 10 per cent and used the proceeds to buy shares in its bank;

2. the rate of return on equity required by shareholders of private banks is 12 per cent. Since the private bank must pay corporate taxes of 50 per cent it must earn a gross rate of return on equity of 24 per cent; and

3. the provincial bank has grown to the point where it has a 20:1 assets to equity ratio.

Under these assumptions, the provincial government would 'break even' in the sense of earning enough to pay the interest on the bonds if it earned, net of intermediation and deposit costs, an average of 0.5 percentage points on each dollar of the $200 million in assets held. On the other hand, a private bank of the same size would have to earn a before-tax margin of 1.2 percentage points per asset dollar in order to provide shareholders with a 'competitive' rate of return. Thus, in this simplified example, because the provincial bank has a lower earnings requirement and pays no taxes it could shave private bank lending rates by seven-tenths of one per cent.[3] Although this example abstracts from all portfolio composition, accounting and tax complexities it offers a dramatic illustration of the lending rate advantage that a provincial bank would enjoy over private institutions.[4]

Among other things, the example ignores the probability that a private bank would be affected differently by acquisition of an abnormally risky selection of assets than would a provincial bank. An increase in the riskiness of a private bank's asset portfolio, other things being equal, would be translated into an increase in risk to its deposit holders and owners. Typically a private bank would have to compensate for this by demanding higher interest rates on the more risky assets and passing along a higher rate of return to its shareholders and deposit holders. In the case of a government-owned bank the government has a greater capacity to accept risk without the need to demand higher rates of return. Presumably, the government is willing to accept the lower rates of return caused by losses and it could, if necessary, finance net losses out of general revenues (thus giving the bank an explicit subsidy). The government guarantees the solvency of the bank and hence the quality of its deposits. A provincial bank is a government guaranteed bank. The implication once again for the pricing policy of the bank is that interest rates required on risky loans can be less than in the case of private banks.

Return, risk and tax advantages

The above analysis suggests that, while lower lending rates may be consistent with government economic and social objectives, the technical ability of a provincial bank to offer them while permitting a provincial government to break even on its investment arises from three factors: the willingness of the government to accept a relatively low required rate of return on equity; preferred corporate tax treatment afforded to crown corporations; and the implicit willingness of the provincial government to assume much of the portfolio risk inherent in the bank's portfolio of assets.

Subsidies to borrowers

These conclusions lead to several other observations. First, lower lending rates offered by a provincial bank may involve a tax subsidy to its borrowers. This should be recognized as such. Borrowers from a private bank must pay sufficiently high rates of interest to permit the bank to earn a competitive rate of return on equity after payment of corporate taxes. Such borrowers, in effect, provide a source of federal and provincial government tax revenues. It follows that any reduction in taxes paid to the government by the banks or other banking type institutions which is due to borrowers taking advantage of lower interest rates at a provincial bank must be recouped elsewhere (assuming that the government revenue requirements remain the same). Either personal, corporate or indirect taxes will have to be increased or more government debt issued. Since corporate taxes on profits earned by a bank in a particular province go to the federal government, the burden of subsidizing lending rates in a given province is partially shifted to residents and corporations in the rest of Canada. Should intergovernmental tax sharing arrangements be such that provincial revenues subsequently fall, provincial tax rates within the province concerned may have to rise.

Profits and provincial bank costs

From the earlier discussion of the nature of bank profits it is apparent that the ability of a provincial bank to realize profit targets will be greater the lower are its per unit intermediation costs. While a few cost reducing factors can be listed, there are also a number of readily apparent cost increasing factors. On the cost reducing side, the ability of a provincial bank to offer customers preferred interest rates could, to some extent, eliminate the necessity for advertising and other promotional expenditures. Sacrifices in the quality of provincial bank branches and other operating facilities might hold down intermediation costs.

Among those factors tending to partially or completely offset such economies would be the need to set up a branch system. Substantial expenditures on plant and equipment would be required. This would mean high per unit capital costs while the bank was small.[5] The high risk policies of the bank would also tend to increase costs. More risky accounts normally generate higher administrative costs because of the need for closer supervision. Losses associated with default on interest and principal payments will also tend to be higher in the case of high risk loans. Low interest rate policies themselves could cause a cost backlash. For example, if low interest mortgage loans were promoted to assist certain low income groups in the province to own homes, the privilege of borrowing at preferred rates would attract borrowers desirous of taking advantage of the government's generosity, even though they don't qualify. Additional expenses associated with policing and screening loan applications would be required to avoid widespread abuse of the bank's programme.

Management efficiency and the incentive system

A further consideration which is difficult to evaluate involves the efficiency of management. It can be argued that if management is fully committed to the goals of the bank they will pursue the bank's business with dedication and efficiency. On the other hand, since long-run profitability has not been proposed as the criterion against which the bank's performance is to be measured, it will be difficult to monitor employee and management performance. This matter of the quality of management decisions also has implications for bank revenues. Will political considerations influence loan authorizations? Since a provincial government controls the bank there may be an incentive for management interested in career advancement to authorize loans which are politically productive even though they are economically unattractive. Thus, the bank could be used by the government to obtain the funds to finance special government projects or purchase provincial government bonds which lie outside the original objectives of the bank. A conflict would exist between the responsibility of the bank to society under its act of incorporation and the needs of the government of the day.

The preceding review of factors which might give rise to higher or lower intermediation costs in a provincial bank compared to existing chartered banks is not intended to be conclusive. Nevertheless, it does suggest that lower intermediation costs should not be counted on as a method of offsetting (or making up for) lower than desired earnings. There is little evidence to suggest that a provincial bank will be more efficient than a private bank.†

From the above analysis it appears that the economic repercussions and thus possible costs to the tax-paying public of a provincial bank would be minimized where it returns to the government sufficient profit to cover financing costs while catering to borrowers not served by private banks. Such borrowers will typically be viewed as high risk by private banks. In such a case a provincial bank would not be a direct drain on government finances nor would it threaten to reduce tax receipts from private banks or other financial institutions.

There is a certain attractiveness to the idea of permitting high risk borrowers to benefit from the ability of a provincial government to capitalize on its financial strength and

---

†Editor's Note: For a discussion of the efficiency of government enterprise, see the essay by Professor Walter Mead, "Private Enterprise, Regulation and Government Enterprise in the Energy Sector," in *Oil in the Seventies,* edited by M. Walker and G.C. Watkins, The Fraser Institute, 1977.

hence preferred position in financial markets, without disrupting private banking operations. Of course, to the extent that a provincial bank does not earn enough to cover the government's financing costs or pulls customers away from private banks, the taxpayers of the province are well advised to ask the government how much owning a bank is going to cost and how such costs are to be financed.

B. Availability and distribution of bank deposits and loans

As an outgrowth of a provincial bank's acceptance of high risk loans, provincial governments hope to achieve changes in the size and geographical distribution of bank loans. To the extent that such indirect benefits arise they should be added to the direct benefits, enjoyed by the borrowers and society, associated with making the loans. However, the following analysis suggests few indirect benefits are in fact likely to arise from pursuing such objectives.

Keeping funds in the province

The analysis of the previous two chapters on the functioning of chartered banks suggests that provincial governments must be careful not to adopt a simplistic approach to the interpretation and determinants of provincial bank deposits and loans. Attempts to keep funds in a particular province constitute a 'beggar my neighbour' type of policy whereby residents of one province would be encouraged to purchase commodities and securities available in their province rather than others. From a marketing and promotional perspective the espousal of a 'keep your funds in this province' policy could be viewed as a marketing technique designed to differentiate the provincial bank's image from those of others operating in the province. Success in differentiating its business from that of other banks would facilitate growth of its share of the deposit and hence lending market. This is not necessarily equivalent to a net increase in deposits or loans to residents of the province. If the customers attracted by the provincial bank's image have been attracted from other provincial deposit-taking institutions such as credit uinions, then the size of the latter would fall at the expense of the former.

Provinces are unlikely to benefit from a campaign to keep funds in the province. Perhaps the gravest danger is that other provinces may retaliate. Interprovincial trade and savings flows would be disrupted. The economic and social benefits Canada enjoys from comparatively uninhibited commodity and deposit flows among the provinces would be placed in jeopardy.[6]

Improve intra-regional balance of deposits and loans

There is some ambiguity about the benefit anticipated by provincial governments from achieving 'a better balance between loans and deposits among all regions' of a province.[7] Insofar as the latter objective is predicated on a desire to achieve social and economic benefits by offering more credit at lower rates to high risk borrowers in rural and northern regions, it has implicitly been taken into account in the discussion. Insofar as it is based on the view that, when deposits exceed loans in a particular community, the balance of loans and deposits is 'unfair' to the community then the implication is that the chartered banks are discriminating against such communities. Expressed another way, provincial governments apparently believe that there is something intrinsically 'good' about banks using funds raised in a particular community for loans in that region.

Much of the analysis of Chapters II and III applies to this matter of intra-regional distribution of deposits and loans. The chartered banks are not concerned with the latter *per se*, nor do they control it. There are serious difficulties in interpreting bank balance sheet data. Funds used in Kitimat in northern British Columbia may arise from a loan booked in Vancouver by the Vancouver head offices of corporations with plants in Kitimat. Thus, more loans may be made to northern or rural regions than is suggested by simply looking at loans on the books of local bank branches in those areas. Surely the relevant concern is whether existing banks and other financial institutions are adequately serving the legitimate credit needs of the various communities and regions of a province, within the limits imposed by their risk/rate of return preferences. It should also be pointed out that deposit holders in those communities are benefitting from being easily able to obtain high quality deposit instruments on which they earn the going rate of interest at existing banks. Even if a bank makes relatively few loans in a particular community, the bank is still serving the saving and payments needs of residents of the community. It is relevant to speculate that such deposit holders would not be sympathetic to high risk regional lending policies on the part of private banks. The consequence could well be insistence by shareholders upon a higher rate of return to compensate the shareholders for greater exposure to risk which, in turn, could mean lower interest rates, higher fees and service charges for deposit holders.

Is loan-deposit balance desirable?

A provincial bank which accepted responsibility for maintaining a close balance between deposits and loans after adequate allowance for cash and liquid asset reserves would probably encounter severe difficulties in implementing such a policy. Ignoring the need to hold reserves, suppose a provincial bank branch in a northern community achieved the 'bliss' state where loans almost equal deposits. What would happen if a resident wanted to increase his loan at his local branch? The ability of the provincial bank to make the loan would depend on the existence of enough deposits on the books of a branch in another community. If the loan is made, is the branch being unfair to the latter? What would happen if a resident moved from the northern community to Vancouver transferring a sizable deposit out of the local branch? If the local branch adhered to a 'loans must equal deposits rule' it would have to call in loans or attract more deposits. Transactions and administrative costs would be incurred. Because they are not particularly concerned about the geographic distribution of their loans and deposits, private banks avoid these sorts of adjustment problems. Such an attitude also permits them to avoid the need to discriminate between communities in the terms and conditions attached to loans.

It should be clear that the residents of a province would not benefit in general from strict adherence to some type of regional or community loan/deposit rule by a provincial bank. A provincial bank should be prepared to lend available funds to borrowers who satisfy its criteria of social need and credit worthiness regardless of the relative size of loans and deposits in the communities concerned.

C. Reducing the general level of bank lending rates

Another aspect of the credo of provincial banking which has been enunciated by provincial governments is that benefits will accrue to a province if a provincial bank is successful in competing down the general level of bank lending rates in the province. The concern here is that the residents of the province are being 'ripped off' by powerful national financial institutions, especially the banks. The 'rip off' takes the form of being charged interest rates on loans sufficiently high to provide private banks with 'excess' profits.

The discussion in Chapters II and III of interprovincial discrimination suggests that banks do not discriminate interprovincially. Thus, bank earnings in one province are unlikely to be excessive relative to rates of return earned in others. Even if it could be proved that profits in banking generally exceed rates of return in other types of financial intermediaries, no explicit intervention by government is required as long as those other intermediaries are able to expand into lending markets served by the banks, thereby over time competing away above normal profits. Profits signal the public's desire for an expansion in banking services. However, expansion of such services takes time. Various competing institutions will only gradually and prudently alter their lending policies to take advantage of new loan market opportunities. However, the purpose of this section is not to argue about whether private bank profits are excessive. It is to analyze the consequences of a provincial bank attempting to lower general lending rates in a province.

Would provincial banks compete away profits?

Provincial governments which have stressed the need for more competition to reduce bank lending rates have not adequately analyzed the probable economic consequences of such a policy. That a provincial bank could probably offer lower lending rates than private banks seems likely in light of the tax and risk advantages it would enjoy. However, in any analysis of the implications of adopting a low lending rate policy, two important considerations should be taken into account. First, as was stressed in Chapter II, private banks are, in general, unable to demand different interest rates from borrowers who are the same in all respects except location (e.g., in Winnipeg and Regina). Hence, a decision to reduce lending rates in one province must be associated with a corresponding reduction in rates in the rest of the country. Secondly, it is the deposit side of the market which holds the key to the ability of a provincial bank to threaten private banks.

A new provincial bank could offer both lower lending rates and higher deposit rates. The lower lending rates would precipitate a surge in loan demand as borrowers interpret the lower rates as a signal of excess lending capacity. The funds to handle the loan demand would be attracted to the bank by higher deposit rates. As deposits switch to the provincial bank it would begin cutting into the deposit and loan market shares of private banks.

Private banks may not respond by matching the rates posted by the provincial bank. Obviously profits would be reduced by doing so. But the critical question is, would profits be hurt more by maintaining interest spreads and losing business in the province or, by reducing the spread between deposit and lending rates across the country. In either case private bank profits would fall and the objective of the provincial government would be realized. A number of considerations should be taken into account when evaluating the desirability of such a policy.

Banking is a low margin, high volume business

The general public would probably not regard the magnitude of the interest rate changes involved as large. Banking in Canada is a high volume, low margin business. A combined increase in deposit rates and fall in lending rates by an average of one percentage point would wipe out the total profits of the banks, before tax and before appropriations for losses. A decline in bank interest rate spreads of one-half of one percentage point would reduce revenues by the amount of their after-tax profit.[8] Obviously, if private banks are earning excess profits small adjustments in interest rates would wipe them out—probably less than one or two-tenths of one per cent. And there is no consensus on whether they are earning excess profits. The Economic Council of Canada concluded after a study of the market power and profitability of the banks that "... the major beneficiary is not so much the bank shareholders as the Government of Canada through its taxes."[9] The major danger is that the provincial bank in its enthusiasm to carve out a share of the bank market might over-estimate the size of the interest rate changes required to turn supposed 'excessively' profitable private banking operations in the province into normally profitable ones. The prospect of inappropriately large changes in rates might be enhanced if the customers of private banks prove to be unresponsive to slight interest rate differentials. Such a miscalculation could have serious consequences.

Low rates for special cases

Of course, a provincial bank could choose to concentrate lower rates on a small segment of their asset portfolio, maintaining rates similar to those of private banks on the rest. This would seem appropriate if certain loans were deemed to be of higher priority than others. Suppose excess profits in private banks amount to 0.2 percentage points of total assets. By confining preferred rates to only one-fifth of its asset portfolio a provincial bank could offer on those assets a one percentage point discount from private bank rates. The question then would be whether a provincial bank is justified in competing with private banks over the eighty per cent of its asset portfolio on which no significant advantage is offered or benefit derived.

All financial institutions will be affected

While a provincial bank is ostensibly concerned with solving problems the government perceives in the operations of the banking system, all banking type institutions will be affected by its low interest rate policies. To the extent that it pro-

motes loans to high risk borrowers, the private lending institutions most severely affected could be consumer loan
and sales finance companies. In general, these institutions
accept higher risk loans than the banks and charge higher interest rates to compensate for that higher risk. It is also
possible that the activities of a government bank could
prove to be a threat to credit unions. The image and philoso-
phy of a government bank—concern about social welfare
and promotion of a provincial, regional or community image—would seem to compete more directly with the co-
operative image of the credit unions than with the big business image of nationally-chartered banks. Deposit and loan
market shares of other intermediaries like trust companies
would also be threatened by an aggressive full service provincial bank.

Near banks not able to earn normal profits as a consequence of competition from a provincial bank would no
longer have an incentive to remain in operation in the province. In such cases it can be anticipated that some provincial
intermediaries might wind up their operations. Nationwide
trust and mortgage loan companies could, like the banks, be
expected to find it unattractive to maintain previously
achieved levels of lending activity in the province.

The tax cost of subsidies

A consideration which may act to restrain the aggressive-
ness of a provincial bank would be the impact of a 'too low',
'no' or 'negative' profit rate on the government's financial
situation and on taxpayers of the province. Higher deposit
rates and lower lending rates squeeze profits. Sufficiently
low profits will reduce earnings below the level required to
cover the cost of financing the government's equity position
in the bank.

Nor would a provincial bank be immune to the dis-
cipline inherent in operating as only one part of the comparatively huge Canadian financial system. If the bank's
interest rates were attractive relative to those available at private institutions, it would be inundated by out-of-province
deposits and requests for loans. The taxpayers of the province might find themselves subsidizing lenders and bor-

rowers in the rest of the country. The attempt to confine interest rate benefits to residents of the province would require more stringent screening and policing procedures. Intermediation costs would rise as would the drain on the provincial government's treasury.

D. A brief recapitulation

If one accepts the proposition that the private chartered banks in Canada are reasonably competitive in the sense of not earning substantial excess profits, then the ability of a provincial bank to offer more attractive interest rates arises from its acceptance of low profits, a preferred tax situation, and perhaps that it can share loan risk with the provincial government. Moreover, few net benefits can be expected from the pursuit of such indirect or ancillary objectives as keeping funds in the province, altering regional loan/deposit ratios, or, to recall the analysis of previous chapters, attempting to overcome interprovincial discrimination by private banks. Concern over the latter issues seems largely unjustified.

Thus, the burden of justification for provincial banking must be borne almost solely by the direct benefits anticipated from government involvement in the processes of financial intermediation in a province (and hence of the country).[10] The next section examines more closely some relevant aspects of those benefits with a view to establishing whether or not they justify the potential costs of provincial banking.

III. PROVINCIAL BANKING AND SOCIAL AND ECONOMIC WELFARE

In general terms the primary benefit expected to flow from the establishment of a provincial bank is that the credit requirements of the province will be better fulfilled. Loan requirements which are unattractive to private banks but which are expected to yield net short and long-term social and economic benefits will be satisfied. The critical question is whether such lending opportunities do in fact exist. And, if they do, whether they are sufficiently worthwhile. Is it important to provide individual persons, households, small businesses and local communities, etc. who do not meet private bank credit standards with the opportunity of enjoying a higher rate of spending now through easier credit requirements and interest rates at a provincial bank? Whether or not low income people should be subsidized is really a question in income distribution and social welfare, about which economics has little to say except to stress that costs may be incurred. However, it is clear that if there is a desire to change the existing distribution of income, setting up a provincial bank is not an efficient and effective way to accomplish this.

An instrument for economic development?

Quite apart from a desire to use the banking system to redistribute income, the provincial governments also view provincial banks as instruments for accelerating the pace of industrial diversification and development. They appear to believe that the latter confer benefits to the economy beyond the direct benefits associated with making the particular loans. An externality exists. One possible rationale is that an increase in the industrial diversification of a provincial economy would lower the risk associated with investment in the province. This might, in turn, stimulate more business investment and spur the growth of the provincial economy to the benefit of the residents of the province.

It is not clear that provincial banking is a valid approach to the promotion of economic development. The provincial bank could simply be treating the symptoms of a high risk economy, not the causes. The reason why the economy is not diversified nor the regions developed probably lies with basic economic difficulties such as a small population and hence market, high transportation costs, high tariffs abroad, or lower worker productivity, etc. Simply subsidizing interest rates is unlikely to achieve much success in offsetting such economic disadvantages. The problems should be attacked directly. There is also an inherent danger in subsidizing interest rates. The borrowers and businesses may never become efficient or self-sufficient. Loans may never be paid off. A provincial bank could inadvertently act to condone inefficiency among a province's industrial firms.

Of course, all provincial governments have welfare, loan, grant and subsidy programmes of various types in operation which are presumably designed to promote the sorts of economic and social goals discussed above. What then does banking offer a provincial government in terms of its ability to deal with a province's economic problems which other forms of intervention do not?

One possible advantage has been alluded to by provincial governments. It is that existing programmes could be brought together under the aegis of the provincial bank and administered through the bank's branches. It may also be the case that as the bank grew existing schemes which involve government lending could be funded using the deposit funds of the bank. However, such administrative efficiencies are unlikely, by themselves, to warrant the establishment of a bank. Perhaps more important from the government's perspective would be the ability of lending programmes financed through the bank to grow more or less automatically with the provincial financial system. This would also seem to offer the prospect of removing lending programmes from close scrutiny by the provincial legislature. A provincial bank would also permit the government to directly control a pool of funds many times its initial investment. The overall financial power of the government, and perhaps its influence in the economy, would rise.

IV. PROVINCIAL BANKING AND MONETARY POLICY

Would the establishment of a new provincial bank (or banks) threaten the ability of the federal government, through the Bank of Canada, to achieve its monetary policy objectives? In 1973, the premiers of the western provinces gave this possibility short shrift. The Canadian Bankers' Association, on the other hand, has expressed considerable concern, while the federal government has been silent on the question.

Monetary policy as it is currently being exercised in Canada emphasizes management of the cash reserves of the chartered banks as the primary method of achieving money supply, interest rate and macro-economic policy goals. By increasing or reducing the amount of reserves available to the banking system, relative to the banking system's required and desired levels, the Bank of Canada can initiate easier or tighter financial conditions, respectively. For example, if the Bank of Canada is stingy with reserves the resulting scramble by banks will push short-term interest rates up. If the banks find themselves persistently short of cash, both deposit and lending rates will tend to rise.

A provincial bank couldn't lean against the financial wind

A provincial bank would have to scramble for cash reserves along with private banks. Even if the bank's response to the general shortage of cash was coloured by concern that the federal government's monetary policy was inappropriate for the province, its ability to hold down lending rates would be constrained by the reluctance of the bank to accept reduced interest spreads and lower profits and the possible need to raise taxes or issue bonds to finance the resulting drain on the government's financial position. It has been previously noted that a slight change in interest spreads can drastically affect profits. Thus, it would be difficult for a provincial bank to lean much against federally-induced changes in the general level of interest rates. Certainly, changes of interest rates of one per cent or more could be expected to force a provincial bank to react in the desired direction. A provincial bank would probably not be a significant threat to monetary policy. It should also be noted that provincial governments can institute a whole range of fiscal and financial measures to counteract federal policies quite apart from a provincial bank. Since federal macro-economic policies require acquiescence or support from provincial governments to be as effective as possible, the matter is better examined in the broader context of whether provincial and federal fiscal and financial policies are consistent and reinforcing in direction and magnitude. This is beyond the scope of this study.

V. PARTIAL PROVINCIAL OWNERSHIP OF BANKS: THE BANK ACT PROPOSAL

Although the above analysis assumed 100 per cent government ownership of a provincial bank it could be applied with only slight modifications to provincial government near banks such as those proposed by the governments of British Columbia and Manitoba. As the Bank Act is written currently, provincial governments are limited to ownership of a maximum of 10 per cent of the non-voting shares of chartered banks. If federal proposals in its *White Paper on Banking* are accepted, the Bank Act will be amended during 1978 to permit partial ownership of the voting shares of new chartered banks by provincial governments. Although this chapter has not been directed specifically at those proposals it does offer a basis to evaluate the desirability of this amendment.

The federal proposal is not intended to encourage provincial government control of chartered banks. It is designed to facilitate the establishment of chartered banks which are basically provincial or regional in their operations by offering the opportunity to provincial governments to provide 'seed' money to groups interested in setting up regionally-oriented banks. Provincial government ownership of voting shares would serve as evidence of provincial government confidence and support for the bank while guaranteeing the new bank a market for a substantial portion of its share issue. Investor reluctance to participate in the purchase of shares issued by new provincially-oriented banks would hopefully be overcome.

Provincial governments interested in owning and controlling their own bank may be expected to find the federal proposal unattractive. Certainly the former government of British Columbia decided not to wait to take advantage of this method of becoming involved in the banking system. Instead it set up the British Columbia Savings and Trust. Provincial authority to set up wholly-owned near banks is the 'ace up the sleeve' of provincial governments in the debate over the Bank Act proposals.

Conflicts of interest?

An unattractive feature of the federal proposal from the general public's point of view is that quasi-government banks are likely to encounter greater difficulties with conflicts of interest and associated uncertainty over what the guiding principles of its policies should be—profit maximization or the government's social and economic policies. If under the new proposal provincial governments initially subscribe to the maximum of 25 per cent of a new bank's shares, effective control of the organization will likely be in the government's hands. Other shareholders as individuals or acting in concert are limited to owning a maximum of 10 per cent of bank shares. As government ownership of voting shares falls to 10 per cent of the total, its control will weaken. Whether the government will continue to possess significant influence over bank policy will depend on how widely the other shares are held and how they are voted.

Where a provincial government owns a bank outright there is no uncertainty about its status. It is a government bank and will pursue government policies. Other shareholders, lenders and borrowers are under no delusion as to the objectives, profit and pricing policies and allegiance of the organization. In the partial ownership case, the status of the bank becomes uncertain. The rate of return offered to shareholders would presumably have to be competitive with that available on private bank shares. But the threat exists that the rate of return would be lower and the risk higher if the government uses its voting power to influence bank policies in the directions deemed politically desirable by the government. The problem of conflicts of interest is likely to become much more severe in cases where a provincial government does not have clear control of the bank. Where does the responsibility of management lie—with the private or government shareholders? Uncertainty over partial government ownership could act to subvert the intent of the federal proposal since potential private investors are likely to be apprehensive over the possible deleterious effects of government influence on the new bank's performance.

VI. SUMMARY, CONCLUSIONS AND RECOMMENDATIONS

The primary purpose of this chapter was to evaluate the economic and financial implications of establishing a new provincial bank. This was accomplished by analyzing certain important benefits and costs which might be expected to flow from such a bank. Perhaps the major 'hoped for' effect would be to offer lower, subsidized interest rates to creditworthy, high-risk borrowers. The ability of a provincial bank to offer subsidized rates would be at least partly, and perhaps largely, due to its tax exempt status. A major benefit of this subsidy might be the encouragement of industrial diversification and growth in the province. Net benefits associated with achieving these objectives could be dissipated if a provincial bank extended its activities to include the pursuit of certain invalid objectives. A prime example of the latter would be the objective of keeping funds in the province. Such an objective reflects a misunderstanding of the operations of the private banks and of the highly integrated nature of the Canadian financial system.

Taken in total, the objectives enunciated by the governments of the western provinces at the Western Economic Opportunities Conference which were subsequently succinctly set forth in the legislation establishing the British Columbia Savings and Trust Corporation, constitute a blanket condemnation of the operations of private banks. The inclusion of invalid objectives along with valid objectives obfuscates the whole issue, which is perhaps what the western premiers were trying to accomplish. It follows that it would be an error to encourage provincial governments to set up banks designed to rectify all of the inadequacies provincial governments attribute to the existing private banking system.

The need for a new provincial government bank should be judged on the contribution it would make to the processes of financial intermediation in the province, taking carefully into account its ramifications for other provinces. Would a new provincial bank add to the efficiency with which funds are channelled from lenders to borrowers? Probably not, with the exception of potential, though negligible, internal administrative gains mentioned earlier. Would a provincial bank offer savings or payments vehicles which are qualitatively superior to those of existing institutions? Because of the risk bearing capacity of a provincial government compared to a private bank some small marginal gains may be possible here. But it must be recognized that small lenders have their bank deposits protected by the Federal Deposit Insurance Corporation and Canadian banks are regarded as extremely safe by North American standards. Would a provincial bank serve to fill in a gap in the capital markets involving an absence of credit at less than prohibitive rates for employment in socially or economically productive activities? It is not clear to what extent such a gap exists given the extensive nature of existing programmes which range from preferred private bank rates for small businesses in the less developed regions of Canada to the lending programmes of the industrial development corporations of the various provinces. Demonstration of the existence of such a gap combined with adherence to the view that industrial diversification and development is good and can be achieved through provincial bank lending would go a long way towards justifying the establishment of a provincial bank.

As mentioned, the size of any net benefits flowing from a provincial bank are likely to decline as it moves beyond gap-filling operations to such subsidiary objectives as reducing the general level of lending rates to wipe out alleged excess private bank profits. Even if the bank operated as an institution specializing in loans to high risk borrowers net taxes would tend to rise in the province if the rate of return was insufficient to at least compensate the government for the cost of equity investment. Extension of its activities to involve competition with private banks across a wide range of loans would generate unavoidable repercussions, probably harmful for near banking institutions as well as private banks within the province. The size and composition of interprovincial flows of funds would also be disturbed. Any policies of a provincial bank which differentially affect the terms and conditions on which credit is available in one province compared to others will have implications for borrowers and lenders in other provinces. The banking system as it currently exists is designed to serve all of Canada in a non-discriminatory manner. Attempts by a provincial government to interfere with its operations so as to achieve discrimination in favour of one province will obviously have implications for the rest of the provinces.

The analysis in this book has ignored many political, philosophical and emotional considerations associated with government intervention in the private sector. These factors may be expected to influence such things as the government's and public's view of the value of the benefits to be derived from subsidized interest rates and the advantages to be gained by being able to do business with a government bank. Some private citizens may attach low weights to potential benefits. They will tend to display a preference for government activities which offer the prospect of lower taxes or higher private business profits now and over the longer term. Judgements about the efficiency with which a government bank will perform its intermediation function is susceptible to philosophical and political bias. The government will be optimistic, confident in the ability of its bank management to operate prudently, sympathetically, independently of political pressures and without conflicts of interest. The business community may be expected to be skeptical of the ability of a provincial bank to operate without higher intermediation costs and to be pessimistic about the possibility of avoiding costly abuses, conflicts of interest and the dangers inherent in the formal extension of the financial power of the government into the banking arena.

The proposed amendment of the Bank Act to permit partial government ownership of bank voting shares is not a satisfactory response to provincial government demands for direct involvement in their province's financial intermediation system. It does not guarantee provincial government control over policy formulation in the provincial bank. This doesn't mean that permitting majority control would be a preferred solution. Of particular relevance here is that provincial government criticisms have been directed at the intermediation activities of banks, not at the important role banks perform as payments institutions. Permitting provincial governments to control banks which have responsibilities in both areas seems more generous than their concerns require.

An alternative proposal would be to permit provincial governments who so desire to establish provincially-incorporated Treasury Branches. Certainly the existence of the latter in Alberta combined with the authority of provinces over provincially-incorporated near banks are two glaring realities which must be taken into consideration in any viable resolution of the debate. However, it may be desirable for the federal government to retain some type of legislative authority over the operations of provincial government-owned banks or near banks. A determined but reckless provincial government bank probably could adopt interest rate policies which would result in persistent, significant interprovincial differences in the general cost and availability of credit. This would interfere with the normal flow of funds within the country and, if pursued to the extreme, could jeopardize the profitability of existing chartered banks and other financial banking type institutions, especially those which lack provincial diversification. The Canadian financial system would suffer.

The challenge then is to devise an institution which would permit provincial governments to enter certain aspects of the banking business so that they can pursue their valid intermediation goals while simultaneously removing the institution as a potential threat to the existing institutions and the stability of the Canadian financial system. A possible solution would be to permit provincial governments to establish provincial banks under federal legislation separate from the Bank Act in the same way that the Federal Business Development Bank is handled. Restrictions could be placed on the functions and operations of such provincial banks to permit them to perform a gap-filling intermediation function without competing with existing institutions in credit markets presently regarded as adequately served. In addition such a provincial bank's asset growth might be linked to net earnings performance. This would impose a limitation on the ability of the institution to take unfair advantage of its provincial government backing to engage in disruptive interest rate policies.

To ignore the desire and right of provincial governments to involve themselves in the process of financial intermediation would be folly. Suitable accommodation must be achieved. Since current federal Bank Act proposals are inadequate, the federal government should prepare new legislation permitting provincial governments to establish and control banks of a different genre from private chartered banks. These new banks should be designed to meet provincial needs and aspirations while avoiding the threat of disruption to the Canadian payments and financial flows.

Notes

[1]Thus no attempt is made to evaluate the benefits and costs associated with the centralization of government cash management operations or the implications of a provincial bank for the development of a province's money market. The controversial issues seem to involve the retail side of the banking business.

[2]One method of attacking in detail questions about the size and nature of costs and benefits of provincial banking might be to study the record of the Alberta Treasury Branches. The stumbling block is that it would be difficult to predict what the province's financial system and economy would have been like in the absence of the Treasury Branches. For example, would credit unions have grown more rapidly in Alberta than they have? And, if so, would the residents of the province been better off?

[3]Alternatively, a provincial bank would be able to offer higher interest rates on its deposits than private banks and might be expected to do so if, for any reason, it experiences difficulty in attracting deposits. Indeed one might argue that the deposit holders of the province should benefit from a provincial bank's pricing policies, just as borrowers do. However, the major thrust of provincial government banking policies has been towards lower lending rates rather than higher deposit rates.

[4]This tax advantage is the same as that enjoyed by credit unions who are not required to pay corporation taxes on earnings distributed to shareholders.

[5]Concern over such considerations as these probably underlies the overtures by the former British Columbia government to use credit union facilities in marketing the British Columbia Savings and Trust.

[6]The Alberta Treasury Branches are predicated partly on the supposed desirability of a resident restricting his deposit holdings to those of provincial institutions. The British Columbia Savings and Trust Corporation may be an example of how such policies tend to spread.

[7]Quote is from a brochure entitled *British Columbia Savings and Trust* issued by the former N.D.P. government of British Columbia.

[8]How realistic are these figures? Some data on the operations of the banks for 1975 may be helpful. During fiscal 1975 Canadian chartered banks recorded gross before-tax profits of $1,031.6 millions or about 0.98 per cent on total assets of $105.3 billions. The banks paid $571 million or about 0.54 per cent of total assets in federal corporate income tax. Thus the balance available for distribution as dividends and building up shareholders equity was $461 million, 0.44 per cent.

[9]Economic Council of Canada, *Efficiency and Regulation,* 1976, p. 47.

[10]Canadian chartered banks are involved in the country's payments system as well but provincial governments have not paid much attention to the payments activities of banks. Presumably this reflects general satisfaction with the way private banks perform their payments function.

Fraser Institute
Books in Print

OIL IN THE SEVENTIES:
Essays on Energy Policy

Edited by **G. Campbell Watkins,** President, DataMetrics Limited, Calgary and Visiting Professor of Economics, University of Calgary and **Michael Walker,** Research and Editorial Director, the Fraser Institute, Vancouver.

In Part One, *Energy in the Marketplace,* contributors include **Russell S. Uhler** of the University of British Columbia (on economic concepts of petroleum energy supply); **Ernst R. Berndt** of the University of British Columbia (on Canadian energy demand and economic growth); and **G. Campbell Watkins** (on Canadian oil and gas pricing).

In Part Two, *Government in the Marketplace,* contributors include **Walter J. Mead** of the University of California, Santa Barbara (on private enterprise, regulation and government enterprise in the energy sector); and **Edward W. Erickson** of North Carolina State University and **Herbert S. Winokur, Jr.,** of Harvard University (on international oil and multi-national corporations).

In Part Three, *Oil in the Seventies: Policies and Prospects,* contributors include **G. David Quirin** and **Basil A. Kalymon,** both of the University of Toronto (on the financial position of the petroleum industry) and **James W. McKie** of the University of Texas at Austin (on United States and Canadian energy policy).

320 Pages   •   17 Charts   •   25 Tables   •   Index
$3.95 paperback ISBN 0-88975-011-4 $14.95 hardcover ISBN 0-88975-018-1

★ ★ ★

FRIEDMAN ON GALBRAITH
. . . and on curing the British Disease

Why is it that the economic mind behind the Prime Minister has few, if any, followers in the economics profession? Why is it that **John Kenneth Galbraith's** theories have become widely accepted when there is a total lack of support for them? Is Galbraith a *scientist* or a *missionary*? **Milton Friedman,** Nobel Laureate in Economics 1976, addresses these and other questions about Galbraith as economist and prophet in this Fraser Institute book. Whatever the reader's view of Galbraith, this book by Friedman is must reading. It is said that Canada and other countries are on the same path as Britain — to some, the *British Disease* is the logical ending of Galbraith's story. In the second essay in this book, Professor Friedman outlines a cure for the British Disease: the principles that Friedman develops in this essay are of immediate Canadian interest as they point out the necessity to adopt gradualist corrective policies *now* before the more jarring policies currently required in the U.K. are necessary here.

66 Pages   • $3.95 paperback   •   ISBN 0-88975-015-7

THE ILLUSION OF WAGE AND PRICE CONTROL
Essays On Inflation, Its Causes And Its Cures

A look at the causes of inflation and an examination of responses to it in Canada, the United States and the United Kingdom. Contributors include **Jack Carr, Michael Darby, Jackson Grayson, David Laidler, Michael Parkin, Robert Schuettinger** and **Michael Walker.**

258 Pages   •   16 Charts   •   7 Tables
$5.95 paperback ISBN 0-88975-001-7 $2.95 pocketbook ISBN 0-88975-005-X

WHICH WAY AHEAD?
Canada after Wage and Price Control

Fifteen well-informed Canadian economists assess the controls programme, suggest the reasons why it should be ended, and propose policies that should be adopted after controls end — **policies to give Canada a healthy and internationally competitive economy — policies for restraint in the public sector — policies to meet the critical double-headed challenge of low inflation and full employment.** Contributors are: **Doug Auld, Jack Carr, Louis Christofides, Tom Courchene, James W. Dean, John Floyd, Herb Grubel, John Helliwell, Stephan Kaliski, David Laidler, Richard Lipsey, Michael Parkin, Simon Reisman, Grant Reuber** and **Michael Walker.**

376 Pages • 5 Charts • 9 Tables • $4.95 paperback • ISBN 0-88975-010-6

★ ★ ★

HOW MUCH TAX DO YOU REALLY PAY?
Introducing The Canadian Consumer Tax Index

Have you ever stopped to think what you pay your federal, provincial, and municipal governments in taxes? Have you ever wondered how much hidden tax you pay on all of the things you buy? This Fraser Institute Guide asks and answers two basic questions: Q: Who pays for government? (A: You do!) and Q: How much do you pay? By reading this book, you will see for the first time how astronomically the Canadian CONSUMER TAX INDEX has risen over the past fifteen years. And if you want to, you can actually calculate how much tax you really pay and your real tax rate.

120 Pages • 6 Charts • 22 Tables • $2.95 paperback • ISBN 0-88975-004-1

★ ★ ★

THE REAL COST OF THE BC MILK BOARD
A Case Study In Canadian Agricultural Policy

Two Simon Fraser University professors of economics, **Herbert Grubel** and **Richard Schwindt,** analyze the social cost of the B.C. milk marketing board, the impact of the milk quota system and the extent to which the Board transfers income from consumers to producers. Grubel and Schwindt develop an analytical framework that can be applied to marketing boards in general. Their study documents the consequences of marketing boards and has been published to stimulate public discussion of the important economic issues at stake.

78 Pages • 6 Charts • 6 Appendices • $3.95 paperback • ISBN 0-88975-013-0

★ ★ ★

PUBLIC PROPERTY?
The Habitat Debate Continued

Essays on the price, ownership and government of land. Edited by **Lawrence B. Smith,** Associate Chairman, Department of Political Economy, University of Toronto and **Michael Walker,** Research and Editorial Director, The Fraser Institute, Vancouver.

Twelve Canadian economists examine the operation and importance of land markets and the impact of government regulation, control and ownership on the supply and price of land. Essential reading for all those concerned with the future of landownership in Canada.

Contributors include: **David Nowlan** of the University of Toronto (on the land market and how it works); **Larry R. G. Martin** of the University of Waterloo (on the impact of government policies on the supply and price of land for urban development); **Stanley W. Hamilton** and **David E. Baxter,** both of the University of British Columbia (on government ownership and the price of land); **Jack Carr** and **Lawrence Smith,** both of the University of Toronto (on public land banking and the price of land); **James R. Markusen** and **David T. Scheffman,** both of the University of Western Ontario (on ownership concentration in the urban land market); **Stuart McFadyen** of the University of Alberta and **Robert Hobart** of the Ministry of State for Urban Affairs (on the foreign ownership of Canadian land) and **Michael A. Goldberg** of the University of British Columbia (on housing and land prices in Canada and the U.S.).

278 Pages	•	7 Charts	•	20 Tables

$5.95 paperback ISBN 0-88975-014-9 $12.95 hardcover ISBN 0-88975-017-3

★ ★ ★

RENT CONTROL—A POPULAR PARADOX
Evidence On The Economic Effects Of Rent Control

Eleven essays on the economics of housing in Canada and on the effects of rent control in the United States, the United Kingdom, Austria, France and Sweden by **F. A. Hayek, Milton Friedman, George Stigler, Bertrand de Jouvenel, F. W. Paish, F. G. Pennance, E. O. Olsen, Sven Rydenfelt** and **Michael Walker.**

230 Pages   •   9 Charts   •   28 Tables   • $2.95 pocketbook   •   ISBN 0-88975-007-6

★ ★ ★

ANATOMY OF A CRISIS
Canadian Housing Policy in the Seventies

In this book—a further title in the Fraser Institute Housing Series—**Lawrence B. Smith,** Associate Chairman of the Department of Political Economy at the University of Toronto, and one of Canada's leading urban economists, considers the content and objectives of Federal housing policies from 1935 to the present. His conclusions that 1) housing policy is more and more being used as a vehicle for redistributing income in Canada and 2) that this policy is at the same time destroying the private sector's incentive and ability to supply housing, make the book required reading for everybody concerned with housing in Canada today. The book contains a comprehensive bibliography.

55 Pages   •   7 Tables   • $3.95 paperback   •   ISBN 0-88975-009-2

★ ★ ★

THE DO'S AND DON'TS OF HOUSING POLICY:
The Case of British Columbia

This book is the second in the Institute's on-going housing economics series, the first of which was: "Rent Control—A Popular Paradox". Economist **Raymond Heung's** book is a case study of housing in British Columbia. As well as taking vigorous issue with the methodology and conclusions of the 1975 Jaffary and Runge reports, (issued as a result of a B.C. government-funded Interdepartmental Study), the Heung book provides a useful and detailed framework for housing market analysis, together with an examination of the costs of adopting a housing allowance scheme for British Columbia. This scheme, guaranteeing access to basic accommodation for all residents in the province, would cost less than half as much as current government outlays on housing in the province. The book, written by a former staff member of the government study team, has a message applicable to every province. As such, it should be of interest to everyone concerned with Canadian housing economics.

145 Pages   •   4 Charts   •   28 Tables   • $8.00 paperback   •   ISBN 0-88975-006-8

★ ★ ★

Published by **THE FRASER INSTITUTE,** Vancouver, B.C.

To: The Fraser Institute,
     626 Bute Street,
     Vancouver, British Columbia,
     Canada. V6E 3M1

BOOK ORDER FORM

Please send me:

_____ copies of _____

_____ copies of _____

_____ copies of _____

Please add $1.00 for postage and handling

Enclosed is my payment in full of $ _____ or charge to:

    Visa # _____

Mastercharge # _____

Expiry Date: _____

Signature: _____

Please send me general information about the Fraser Institute . . . . . . ☐

Please send me information about membership in the
    Fraser Institute . . . . ☐

please print

Name: _____

Title: _____

Organization: _____

Address: _____

_____

_____

please include postal code